MW00897851

The Real-Life Story Begins

One Eye Open and One Eye Closed

My Life Story

Linda J. Flarisee

Copyright © 2017 by Linda J. Flarisee

One Eye Open and One Eye Closed
by Linda J. Flarisee

Printed in the United States of America.

ISBN 9781498497565

All rights reserved solely by the author. The author guarantees all contents are original and do not infringe upon the legal rights of any other person or work. No part of
this book may be reproduced in any form without the permission of the author. The
views expressed in this book are not necessarily those of the publisher.

Unless otherwise indicated, Scripture quotations taken from the King James Version
(KJV) – public domain

www.xulonpress.com

Table of Contents

Acknowledgments

I dedicate this book to my dear mom, who was the rock of the family. She passed away on July 22, 2008; she received her heavenly crown.

To my husband, Samuel, my three children (LaTonya, Sherman, and Tammie), my granddaughter (Ashlee), my grandson (Taylor), my great-granddaughter (Aniyah), my six sisters (Donna, Debra, Barbara, Sandra, Pamela, and Patricia), my five brothers (Bobby, David, Anthony, Daniel, and Nathaniel), my sisters-in-law (Janice, Edwina, Brenda, and Kim) and my brothers-in-law (Willie, Eras, and Wayne). I love you all!

I can't thank enough my family and friends who believed in me. You helped my vision come to fruition. Dr. Rueben P. Anderson, First Lady Nettie Anderson, Dr. J.A. Caruthers, Sister Linda Parham, Sister Debra Smith, Evangelist Darlene Nevels, Pastor Calvin Hollins, Pastor Louis Jamison, First Lady Mary Jamison, Pastor Alice Lancaster, Pastor Lisa Coleman-Kincy, Bishop Joe L. Ealy and my church family you all have been instrumental in my life. I cannot forget my best friend, Bridget Smallwood, who always encouraged me with words of wisdom. You have been a blessing to me for over twenty years.

I cannot forget one of my spiritual moms, Mother Blanche Cannick, who always gave me the opportunity to showcase my talent in ministry. Love you!

A Blossom of Love: My Spiritual Mom

T he title of this book was inspired by one of my spiritual moms, Mother Lucy Moore, who spoke a prophetic word to me in 1969. She had a dream that I had one eye open and the other eye closed. I was in my early twenties when she said, "You need to be watchful because Satan is out to destroy your ministry." I was young and did not quite understand the prophecy.

I worked faithfully with my spiritual mom in ministry, who was the founder of the Little People Outreach Ministry. I spent several years fasting, praying, and ministering on the street corners of Skid Row and in Chino's men's prison and Corona's women's prison. My spiritual mom was instrumental in the work I did as I ministered at Fred C. Nelles Youth Correctional Facility as a volunteer once a month. I witnessed hundreds of women, men, and children give their hearts to the Lord.

Mother Moore was a great woman of God; at the age of seventy years old, she was still ministering to the lost. She resided in the city of Watts, where she would launch a tent in her front yard and preach the gospel. Mother and I, along with her daughter, Linda, conducted several revivals under the tent. One of the most exciting events was the baptismal service. Mother Moore used a swimming pool she purchased from the store to baptize several candidates. It was a joyful occasion as we sang songs and praised God for the conversion of so many young men and women.

Mother Moore was a great soul winner, and I am so grateful and appreciative to her for showing me how to be an effective soul winner. She has lived the scripture according to Luke 14:23, "And the Lord said unto the servant, Go out into the highways and hedges, and compel them to come in, that my house may be filled."

Although she has not received the accolades of men, I am confident that she will receive a crown in heaven for being a soul winner. My dear spiritual mom is at the ripe age of ninety years old. I give God the glory for this great woman, **a blossom of love.**

Chapter 1
The Family

To share my feelings is therapeutic to the healing of my own personal struggles, and it starts in my childhood. As a certified drug and alcohol/domestic violence counselor, one of my primary assignments was to evaluate my personal struggles. I became a better person as I began to move, by God's divine love, toward my emotional healing. I understand the value of family.

In spite of my struggles, I have overcome the darkest hours of despair. When I was feeling discouraged and sad, I learned how to pray. My mom, who was instrumental, taught me life skills of how to cope in difficult situations, even though she had a difficult time sharing her own feelings. She never expressed openly how difficult life was, but she prayed about everything.

I grew up in a home comprised of twelve children, with five boys and seven girls. I am the oldest child. We learned how to share early in life because we lived in a two-bedroom house. The garage was converted into a bedroom for my parents.

I remember how crowded the girls' room was, with one set of triple bunk beds. Can you imagine seven girls in one bedroom? I was so frustrated because occasionally the two top beds would fall on me. My sisters would help put the bed back together. Now, the boys did not experience their beds falling. They had two sets of bunk beds. Four of the boys had their own beds, and the baby had to sleep with someone.

Mom was a strict disciplinarian. Mom set rules regarding respecting elders, and she did not tolerate disrespect.

We were not allowed to watch television. Mom and the elderly saints in the church called the television "the one-eyed devil." I just could not understand why we could not look at television. To add more injury to our emotions, the girls weren't allowed to wear pants. I had to wear a skirt during gym class at school. I was so embarrassed. Since miniskirts were in style, I rolled up my skirt as soon as I turned the corner. I had enough sense to know that if my mom caught me, I was going to be in trouble. As I walked home from school, the closer I got to home, I would roll down my skirt. When I arrived home, I would be so glad that I did not get caught wearing a miniskirt.

We could not roam the streets like other children; we learned to play with each other at home. We played baseball, marbles, jacks, ping pong, hide and seek, and tether ball. We climbed trees and hopped fences. The girls would cut out brown paper bags to make paper dolls.

I loved Christmas because it was a time that made you forget about all the bad things you'd experienced. We got a pair of roller skates that had to be worn with shoes. I received so many scars from skating. I had so much fun because we played Roller Derby, and thirty or more kids from the neighborhood would be skating. I enjoyed the time away from home, but I knew when the streetlights came on, we had to be in the house.

Dad was a functional alcoholic, and he made good money. He was self-employed, and he paid cash for a green Cadillac. We were so excited about the car. But our excitement was for a short period, because he started his old behavior of controlling again once. He came home from work after he had been drinking, and made us go to bed at 5:00 p.m., when it was still daylight. We were too afraid to say anything. When he heard us talking in the room, he told us to shut up.

I was confused as a child. I witnessed physical, verbal, and mental abuse. At that time, we did not have a clue that what we were witnessing was domestic violence, and that my dad's behavior was all about power and control. I just thought it was the norm of how a family should be.

My mom did not know that she had become vulnerable to Dad's emotional abuse. She was an extraordinary woman who triumphed over all her trials. She was the glue that kept the family together. I never saw my mom argue with my dad. She was so humble. I saw her praying to God. Although Dad made lots of money, he never gave her enough. She had to learn how to sew to make our dresses. The boys' Sunday attire was nice pants, a shirt, and a nice pair of shoes. They were not allowed to wear tennis shoes on a Sunday.

Since I was the oldest child, it seemed like I was the one being abused the most. Once, when I was in junior high, he came home drunk, woke me up at 2:00 a.m., and told me to get up to clean the kitchen ceiling. Although I was crying, I got on top of the sink and started washing the ceiling. I did not get to bed until 3:00 a.m. I thought he was the meanest person in the world. I was so tired and sleepy the next day. I had to go to school, like nothing ever happened. I isolated myself and did not talk as a way of coping with the abuse.

In the 1970s, we did not discuss abuse. We were taught that what went on inside the house stayed in the house. On Wednesdays, Mom went to the 10:00 a.m. prayer meeting. She testified that she was being abused by her husband. The old mothers in the church put my mom in the circle and began to pray, saying, "By the blood of Jesus, come out of the man. I rebuke you in the name of Jesus; loose Satan and go back to the lake of fire."

Sometimes to keep from getting abused, I would run out of the house at 3:00 a.m. in the morning. My dad, in his drunken stupor, would be chasing me in his old white pickup truck and would say, "I am going to kill you." I would be hopping fences, trying to get away. My brother, who is the third-oldest child, wanted to be my protector, so he would go with me.

I started acting out my feelings. One difficult time in the seventh grade was when my dad hit me in my left eye for no apparent reason. Immediately, my eye swelled, and I had a black eye. I could not go to school. I assumed my mom was afraid, so I called my grandma and she picked me up. She came with her pistol. I loved my grandma; her nickname was Honey. I felt loved and secure with her. My grandma was cool. She loved to party, and she let me party. I stayed with her for approximately two years before my mom did not want me to stay with her any longer. I had to go back home, and I was furious.

Do you think the abuse stopped? No! I still was being abused. I hated my dad, and could not forgive him for hitting me in the eye. How did I cope with the abuse? I rebelled by smoking cigarettes and drinking. I had a hard time coping emotionally. All my self-esteem was being chipped away by my anger. I became exhausted, worn out, and upset because no one came to rescue me. I was confused and distraught; I began to feel unloved, and I had a deep, secret hatred toward my dad. I was emotionally isolated as a teenager. My mom did her best to rebuild what Dad had torn down in me, but I struggled with my emotions.

Does abuse affect the behavior of children? I say yes! Sometimes parents are in denial and say the abuse is a form of correction. When I was a teenager and experienced abuse, I did not see it as a positive form of discipline, especially from my dad. I was beaten with an extension cord and a water hose.

I remember the last harsh experience that occurred when I graduated from high school. I had accepted the Lord Jesus as my personal Savior, and I was so happy because it gave me a sense of peace in the midst of my inner struggles. I had gone in the living room to pray; this was time for me to communicate with God and to share my feelings of despair. My dad came home and saw me praying, and he said, "Get up." I refused to, and kept praying. All of a sudden, he grabbed me by my hair and dragged me across the floor. I started crying hysterically and ran into my bedroom. I cried all night, and I heard the voice of the Lord say, "My child, I have not forsaken you. I will always be with you." This was the beginning of my transformation.

As a teenager, I did not get lots of hugs and kisses. All I heard was repetitive negative comments that Dad would communicate to Mom. Mom did not let it get her down; she focused on her twelve children. Sometimes parents are unaware that they use their children to fulfill their own emotional needs.

My mom was the authoritative figure; she demanded that we respect her, and we were prohibited from disrespecting our dad. Acting out her authoritative role allowed her to vent her feelings of disappointment or frustration, because she was in control of her children.

We did know that our family was dysfunctional. Because of the lack of intimacy and the abuse, some of us had a hard time coping in a positive way—especially me. I felt I was the scapegoat in the family. I was in denial, and I used to blame others for my anger and resentment. I was codependent on the family. I was afraid of commitment. I found myself trying to seek the approval of others. I had to identify my own self-defeating attitude, such as comparing myself with others, and my fear of expressing my feelings. I needed to fill my own emotional needs.

My biggest problem was fear. I had a difficult time expressing myself. I began to transfer my feelings of anger and resentment by internalizing my feelings. I was unhappy, and I hated when my mom made us go to church. We spent our childhood in church; we took up two rows, and we had to sit in the front of the church. My mom sat behind us so she could watch us. We stayed at church for both Sunday school, which began at 9:00 a.m., and Sunday morning worship at 11:00 a.m. We then stayed at church to prepare for the 3:00 p.m. afternoon service, and we did not go home until the after the 8:00 p.m. service was over. Mom seemed to never want to go home to her mean husband. But my mom's attendance at church was only a temporary release, because as soon as she returned home, Dad was in his raging moods. She never tuned into her feelings, and she seemed to acts like life was a wonderful bed of roses. One Sunday, I made the mistake of saying I didn't want to go to church. She said, "As long as you are in my house, you will go to church." That was the last time I made that statement.

Even though she made me go to church, I still did not feel protected and secure. I was silently depressed, and I viewed myself as being unimportant. The abuse impacted my life, and I carried feelings of despair. Mom did not know what to do or say to me, because she also was a victim of abuse. I did not speak of the dark, secret hatred I was experiencing. To fill the void of unacceptance, I became involved in an unhealthy relationship. Because the person was insensitive to my emotional needs, I experienced a poor sense of self-worth. Now my emotions were of inner doubts and insecurities. I learned survival skills as a teenager by being emotionally isolated to ease my pain. Most teenagers have problems with self-disclosure, as do adults.

I went to college and took a class on family dynamics and counseling, and this is when I understood the importance of therapy. I was motivated to change my behavior as I looked within myself. Now I know that it's OK to have disagreements within the family, because this is a part of life. I learned what the triggers of my anger are and how to dismantle those feelings. Since I have self-actualized, I no longer have low self-esteem. I have become independent and self-sufficient, and I focus on my strengths as well as my weakness. I am more confident, and live a well-balanced life.

My testimony is to never give up on your children. I had a brother who was addicted to drugs for ten years, and he refused to admit that he had a problem. My mom was so concern about my brother that when he would go on a binge, she would call us over to her house, whether it was midnight or 2:00 a.m., to look for him. We would go in dangerous neighborhoods, jeopardizing our own safety. I went to school to learn about the disease of drugs and alcohol, and the symptoms of relapse. I studied my brother's behavior, especially how he was unable to verbalize his feelings. When he felt stressed, he disassociated himself from the family to numb his feelings and to escape from his emotional turbulence. My mom kept praying for him, and my brother is now free from drugs and is preaching the gospel.

Another of my brothers got in trouble with the law and went to prison for fifteen years. So many families forget about their love ones who are incarcerated, but my mom said, "This is your brother, and we need to show him love." We visited the penitentiary once a month for fifteen years. My mom sent packages to him faithfully. My brother also told my mom about several inmates who didn't have visitors, so Mom sends all of them packages. How amazing is a mom's love for her son. Today, my brother is doing great, and our love for him helped him overcome this chapter in his life.

Mom had a way of showing us love. She was a good cook. For a long time, I thought liver was steak because she seasoned it so well. We never missed a meal; breakfast, lunch, and dinner were always served.

Finally, Dad stopped drinking; my mom's prayers have been answered. She believed that one day God was going to deliver her husband from alcohol, and He did. We were so happy when he started going to church. He would sit way in the back; Mom had a lot of wisdom, so she didn't bother him.

Our family is now comprised of forty-eight grandchildren, and some of them have already earned their undergraduate, master's, and juris doctorate degrees. Mom was so proud of their accomplishments. She has fifteen great-grandchildren. My son promised my mom that he was going to get his doctorate degree before she passed. The day she passed was the day he was accepted into his doctorate program.

Even though Mom had so many grandchildren, she spent quality time with each one. She would talk to them individually and encourage them to be good students. My mom's faith in God was the glue that kept the family together. One of our family traditions is that whenever a family member gives birth, we all go to the hospital and stay until she delivers. Another tradition is family prayer. This was the time when Mom talked to us and our children. She shared that each child was loved, valued, and cherished as a person. Mom had a way of respecting each child's individuality. She also was a disciplinarian and was deeply committed to her family. Mom had a way of getting the children to communicate effectively. She would chastise you if you had an attitude of selfishness and if you threw tantrums.

We just loved to sit around in the dining room and chat with Mom. She was a woman filled with wisdom. She lived the Bible, and believed that holiness and righteous living is pleasing to God. She was a firm believer in the importance of forgiveness. I have never witnessed another family in which the ex-brothers-in-law come to all the family gatherings. We still have a bond with them, because Mom said, "If you are a Christian, you are supposed to forgive. As long as there are children involved, you have to be an example for your children." My mom never liked drama, so if you have baby mama drama, you would not survive in our family.

Everyone always wanted to be at Mom's house, especially during the holiday season. One of my nieces got married, and her husband's family lived out of town. My mom was not selfish. She told my niece, "You need wisdom, and you cannot be selfish when you are married. Now, this is what you need to do: spend the holiday with his family this year, and next year his family can come to you." The plan worked perfectly, and for the past ten years, they have been rotating their visits. If you listen to the wisdom of my mom, you will make it in your relationship.

We loved to spend time at Mom's house on a daily basis. As soon as we got off work, we would all meet at Mommy's house. The grandchildren loved to visit. I have a few friends whose grandmothers had a problem when the grandchildren came around. A few shared with me that they hated going over to their grandma's house. My mom was unique because she loved company. We always knew we were going to get some good home-cooked food; Mom cooked every day. I was always amazed how Mom could cook enough food for over thirty people, and there was still enough for the neighborhood kids who stopped by.

My mom had her special chair where she would sit and we would laugh and talk. She was serious about the family staying together and being a role model. If you made a mistake, she would forgive you. One thing for sure is that we don't hold grudges with one another. We were not perfect, and with twelve children, you are going to have some disagreements. Sometimes we got into what I called plain old knock-out, drag-out arguments, but before the day was over, we were laughing and talking.

One time, two of my brothers were going at it outside. My mom ran out of the house with a mop, started hitting my brothers with it, and said, "How dare you embarrass me." Immediately, my brothers stopped. Oh, Mom had a problem with you being disrespectful, especially in public. Because of Mom's respectful ways, she did not want my brothers to hurt themselves, and they listened to her. My mother had a major influence on her children. Not long after this episode, my brothers were sitting at the table, playing dominoes. Showing your children that you love them in spite of their mistakes will enforce them to become mentally, physically, and emotionally healthy. When we started getting out of character, she would let you know that God was not pleased. Mom would start praying for you, and would tell you to ask God and the person you offended to forgive you.

My mom taught us to spend time with our children. Although I was a working mom, I went to every football, wrestling, and basketball game. My granddaughter ran track, and I went to every track practice and all-day Saturday track meets, even meets scheduled out of town. Some of my friends were amazed at the patience and support I gave to my children and grandchild. I did it because I knew that if I would help, they would become economically productive and spiritually matured adults.

I am a firm believer that when you are involved with your children, they will not be victims of the negative influences of their neighborhoods.

Mom used to say, "You can live in the ghetto, but the ghetto doesn't have to be in you." Mommy had several pictures on the wall of her children and grandchildren who graduated from high school and college. Some of them have already earned their undergraduate, master's, and juris doctorate degrees. It is something to see; we call it the wall of fame. Mom was proud of the accomplishments of her family, and was very instrumental in moral and financial support. Many people who visit and see all of those pictures are astonished.

We all have our unique personalities. Some of my sisters are gifted with braiding hair, making gift baskets that look like they were purchased from a major store, and organizing for banquets, weddings, and other events. One of my sister can sew, others are great cooks, and others work in professional business in the work field. My brothers' skills are in construction and carpentry. They can cook, and most importantly, they are good providers for their families.

We do what Mom taught us when we became parents, which is to spend time with our immediate family.

My mom was classy, and when we were teenagers, she had all the girls attend the Ebony Fashion Fair. We also loved going to Roller Derby and wrestling matches when we were younger.

We planned family trips with our children; we went to all of the amusement parks, the LA Zoo, the San Diego Zoo, the Ice Capades, and cruises, and we loved taking the boys to wrestling matches and baseball games. The circus was the highlight. We dined at the finest restaurants. We celebrated family members' birthdays, retirements, and wedding anniversaries. Can you imagine forty people together?

We had a blast. We had a great time, especially at the family reunions, because it was five generations of us.

One of my favorite scriptures is Psalms 34:18–19, "The Lord is nigh unto them that are of a broken heart; and saveth such as be of a contrite spirit. Many are the afflictions of the righteous: but the LORD delivereth him out of them all." I witnessed the change in my dad when he stopped drinking alcohol, and I saw how he did everything to restore his love for his family.

He added rooms to the house, and it now has five bedrooms, two baths, and a large dining room. My younger sisters and brothers got to enjoy family life, and thank God they did not have to experience what I went through as a child. The principles I live by are what my mom taught me: to love God, to love your family, to love your church, and to love people. Truly, I am a lover of family and people.

I love Christmas; it is a time that I hold dear to my heart. As I roll back the curtain of memory, I think about Christmas at Mommy's house. We'd bring all the toys and gifts we'd purchased for our children and put them under the tree. Can you imagine all those gifts from twelve children and forty-eight grandchildren being opened? It is a sight to see all the happy faces on Christmas, and everyone thankful for their gifts. Mommy never failed to keep the old tradition that dad started by giving all twelve children, sisters-in-law, and brothers-in-law twenty-five. We knew we were going to get twenty-five dollars from Dad on Christmas. When we saw that envelope, we acted like we are so surprised, even though we knew what was in the envelope. Dad just smiled because he knew we were appreciative.

Christmas at my parents' house was so much fun. We had an essay contest on various topics. One year's topic was "What does Christmas mean to you?" There are three categories: ages eight to ten, eleven to fourteen, and fifteen to seventeen. The winner wins fifty dollars, second place wins twenty-five dollars, and third place wins fifteen dollars. The essay has to be original, and we are training the children in public speaking. We have non-family as judges, and the person who has the most points is the winner. I have some intelligent nieces and nephews.

We play games, and one particular game is called Raging Water. Each person receives a clue to get them closer to the hidden treasure.

The kids all run through the house, trying to find the clue. We have so much fun watching them. The winners win a prize.

The spiritual side of the Christmas season makes you forget about all the bad news you hear about economic crisis. I believe God is working all things for our good; there is not a place I want to be other than with my family on Christmas.

Thank you, Mommy, for your legacy, as you taught us that Jesus is the giver of all good things, and that we should have the same spirit and give love to our family. I have been resurrected emotionally, mentally, and spiritually.

It was sad when my dad's demise came at the age of sixty-three. He was in the front yard, getting ready to cut the grass. Oh my God, that is what he enjoyed doing, and we had the best-looking grass in the neighborhood. Prior to his death, Dad kept saying that he may not always be around; of course, we didn't believe him. He always wore a white uniform, and he did not own a suit. He told my sister that he wanted a suit. They went downtown and purchased a suit. He showed my mom all of the insurance papers, and we laughed. He was not sickly, so we thought he was just talking. Based on what he shared, he knew he was going to die. Dad was talking to my brother, who helps him with the yard. My brother told us Dad said, "Man, I feel like I'm getting ready die."

My brother responded, "Dad, quit playing." He went in the backyard to get the lawn mower, and when he returned, Dad was lying in the yard. He'd had a massive heart attack. I was called from my job to come home because there had been an emergency. When I arrived, I had to try to console my sisters and brothers. My mom got into the ambulance with our father, and when she arrived at the hospital, she was alone. She wondered what had happened to her children. They were so emotional that they had not realized that the ambulance had left with Dad. Finally, they calmed down and went to the hospital. There was a lot of crying. The nurse on duty said she had never seen so many family members at one time.

The day of Dad's funeral, many people came, and we were overwhelmed by the love of so many. Mom was a strong woman and a sharp dresser. She looked pretty as she walked down the aisle into the funeral, blowing kisses to everyone. The Lord gave her strength. She rejoiced and praised God because she was a virtuous woman.

My brother, who is a preacher, was the first to give remarks. He started talking and saying, "If you came to cry, you are in the wrong place, because Dad was saved." As soon as the casket opened he started hollering and got in our mom's lap.

The next day, I teased him, saying, "You cannot represent the family, and you will not be the spokesperson at any of *our* funerals." We all laughed because he is forty years old. I said to my mom, "You walked into the funeral like you were a movie star." She thought that was the funniest thing she had ever heard. We had a good time talking about the funeral.

I was so amazed of how, during the funeral procession, the motor-cyclist shut down the freeway so all the cars could get on. I never saw so many cars going to a cemetery; it was about a hundred cars. For a moment, I thought my dad must have been a movie star or some official in the Senate.

Our family has grown; it is now comprised of seventy grandchildren, twenty great-grandchildren, and one great-great-grandchild. I wrote this book several years ago (it is now 2016), and the family is still together. My mom has been deceased for nearly eight years, and we are still living her legacy. Every Tuesday at 6:00 p.m., I host the family prayer that Mom started forty years ago. We still have our essay contest at Christmas, we go on family trips, we have birthday parties, and our children are doing well in school and graduating with bachelors and master's degrees. To God be the glory!

As a family, we understand the importance of emotional under-standing and healthy support, and our children are able to excel.

Chapter 2
The Old-Fashioned Prayer Meeting

As I roll back the curtain of time, I realize that powerful prayer was indispensable to my mom. She believed that if you are committed to pray, prayer will strengthen your inner man. Matthew 6:9–13 says, "After this manner therefore pray ye: Our Father which art in heaven, Hallowed be thy name. Thy kingdom come, Thy will be done in earth, as it is in heaven. Give us this day our daily bread. And forgive us our debts, as we forgive our debtors. And lead us not into temptation, but deliver us from evil: For thine is the kingdom, and the power, and the glory, for ever. Amen."

My mom attended Wednesday-morning prayer faithfully at ten o'clock in the home of a friend once a week. One particular day, I was over at my best girlfriend's house, around the corner from Mom's house. There was a knock on the door. My girlfriend answered the door, and it was my mom.

She asked, "Shirley, have you seen Linda?"

My friend responded, "Yes, she is right here."

Mom said, "Come on, you are going to prayer."

Oh, I put up a fuss all the way to the prayer meeting. I was so embarrassed that she had come to get me from my girlfriend's house. When we arrived, there were about ten women there who were full of the Spirit. The Spirit of Christ convicted me, and I was so scared that God was going to reveal to those godly saints that I had a package of cigarettes in my purse. I was smoking two packs of cigarettes a day.

My mom had no idea that I was addicted to cigarettes. I said, "Please don't let my mom find out that I have cigarettes in my purse."

I start having flashbacks of when my brother was acting out in school. My mom believed in driving the devil out of you by whipping you with a belt or a switch.

My mom asked my brother, "Why did you do it?"

My brother responded, "The devil made me do it."

My mom said, "Well, I am about to beat the devil out of you."

All of sudden, those saintly mothers gathered around me and started praying, "By the blood of Jesus, come out of her, in the name of Jesus." This generation doesn't know about the old-fashioned prayer meetings. Before I knew it, I was rolling on the floor from one end to another, asking God to forgive me and save me. Immediately, I was filled with the Holy Ghost, with the evidence of speaking in tongues. I left the prayer meeting with a new attitude.

I ran over to my best friend's house and gave her the good news. My friend started crying uncontrollably. She was hurt because she knew that we could no longer party together and drink. If the truth was told, we had a good time partying and drinking together. We were best friends. I told her, "Why don't you join me?"

I was filled with so much joy. When I went to bed that night, I had an out-of-body experience that I would never forget. I felt my sins being pulled out of my system; it was like tug-of-war. I felt my old spirit trying to remain and my new spirit tussling; then, all of sudden I felt a relief, and the Lord said to me, "I am putting a new Spirit in you that will enable you to stand during difficult times." I did not understand what he was saying, because it was all new to me.

The next day, I was telling everyone, "I am saved." I felt like the woman at the well: "Come and see the man who told me all about myself." I was such a character when I got saved that nineteen other teenagers also immediately came to Christ. They said that if God could save Linda, He surely could save them.

My mom started a prayer meeting in our home on Saturdays. The young people from the church would gather, and some of the neighborhood kids also came to fellowship with our family, which was already comprised of twelve children. We called our prayer meeting the Holy Ghost Party; after the prayer, we served hot dogs, chips, and Kool-Aid.

We had a good time fellowshipping with one another. A few of my sisters were gifted to pray, especially Debra, who God used in visions. My brother Bobby was ten years old when he was called to preach. He was also gifted to pray. My sisters Sukie, Donna, and twins Pamela and Patricia *really* knew how to pray. It was amazing how God used them early in their childhood to pray.

I was the missionary in the family, and the Lord used me to lay hands on those who attended the prayer meeting. One particular Saturday, we had nineteen visitors along with my twelve siblings. The anointing of God was upon me as I laid hands on those nineteen teenagers, and immediately they accept Jesus into their hearts. I really didn't know how to properly use my gift, but the Lord knew my heart. I started swinging them so hard that they would fall down, and then I would kneel down beside them and lay hands on them. When Mom came in the room, she thought everyone was slain under the power. Later, I told her I just started swinging them until they fell. It was hilarious after I matured, and now I know God looks at the intentions of our heart. He knew I was young and had no experience, but He saved every last one of those teenagers.

Mom had to travel back and forth to visit her grandmother, who was ill. Mom asked our neighbor Ms. Robinson, who was a schoolteacher, to keep an eye on us. She heard a lot of noise and peeked into the house through the mail slot, and she was shocked to see all twelve of us children on their knees, praying and speaking in tongues. When my mom returned from Fresno, Ms. Robinson told my mother what she had witnessed. My mom was so proud of her children. My mom believed in the old cliché "a family that prays together stays together."

I am a firm believer that prayer changes things, and if you need a character change, prayer will do it. I believe that having a strong character doesn't just happen; it comes from your present and past experiences, and how you are able to handle difficulties in life. To have a prayerful life allows you to overcome the storms of life. You can communicate with God, and He is a good listener.

Prayer changed my life, and if I had not prayed for divine protection and faith to overcome the greatest challenges in my life, I would not have survived. I certainly believe in the scripture in Isaiah 26:4,

"Trust ye in the LORD for ever: for in the LORD JEHOVAH is everlasting strength."

I'd like to share a few scriptures that I love from the King James Thompson Chain Reference Bible. One of my favorites is 2 Chronicles 7:14: "If my people, which are called by my name, shall humble themselves, and pray, and seek my face, and turn from their wicked ways; then will I hear from heaven, and will forgive their sin, and will heal their land."

The prayer that unites us as a family is Matthew 18:19: "Again I say unto you, That if two of you shall agree on earth as touching any thing that they shall ask, it shall be done for them of my Father which is in heaven."

When I was young, I would read Matthew 6:6: "But thou, when thou prayest, enter into thy closet, and when thou hast shut thy door, pray to thy Father which is in secret; and thy Father which seeth in secret shall reward thee openly." I actually got into my closet in my bedroom, and that's where I prayed every day. I thought the Bible was saying to get in a literal closet. Oh, I had some great times in the closet, and that's when the Lord spoke to me and said, "My child, you are going to preach the gospel."

I was eighteen years old when I accepted Jesus Christ as my personal savior. I was a member of a neighborhood church. While a member, I attended Sunday school and sung in the choir. I was faithful to my church, and I had this calling on my life. I was called into ministry. I began to pray, read my Bible, and seek guidance from God. I told my mom that God had called me to ministry. My mom believed that I had this call on my life, because as I said, I was the missionary in the family. It was difficult because in my era, men in the church did not accept the fact that a woman can be called to be a preacher. Now, they would not say you *preach*, but instead they used the term *teach*. I did not argue with them, because I knew God had spoken and anointed me.

During the infancy of my ministry, the Lord led me to walk to the community hospital and pray and minister to the sick on Sunday evening at 7:00 p.m. I would go alone. God called me to be a soul winner. I saw people in the hospital be healed. It was amazing when I would testify. All of a sudden, I started preaching, so my pastor recognized that I had this calling. I attended numerous shut-ins and prayer meetings at the church. This is where I received my humble beginning in ministry. I continued to be faithful, and finally I preached my first message. Of course, they said, "You sure did *teach*." I smiled and went to my seat, because I knew I had preached.

In 1969, I was at my first job out of high school at Security Pacific National Bank. The Lord spoke to me and told me to conduct a revival.

I said, "Lord, where?"

He said, "On Fifth Main Street."

I worked on Fourth Main Street in downtown Los Angeles on Skid Row. I conducted my first revival on Skid Row for one week. I invited my coworkers and I preached, and some received Jesus Christ in their lives. Some of the coworkers were crying. One of my missionary friends came to support me, and it was awesome. Later, God blessed me to join several groups of missionaries, The Rescue Squad and The Missionettes. We were blessed to minister at Chino's men's prison, Fred C. Nelles Youth Correctional Facility, and Corona's Women's Prison. I also ministered on many street corners and park rallies.

We were a group of women who believed in the power of prayer. We believed that once we prayed, we would receive the resurrected power of Jesus. We knew that we were anointed an appointed. For the Bible says in Romans 8:11, "But if the Spirit of him that raised up Jesus from the dead dwell in you, he that raised up Christ from the dead shall also quicken your mortal bodies by his Spirit that dwelleth in you."

I believe that whenever you pray, God will answer you according to His will. I can testify that forty years have gone by, and we still have family prayer each Tuesday at my Mom's house. We are carrying the legacy of our dear saintly mom. She taught us to pray, to not give up on your loved ones, and that there is life after a divorce or the loss of a spouse.

Another favorite scripture of mine is Psalm 91:15: "He shall call upon me, and I will answer him: I will be with him in trouble; I will deliver him, and honour him." When you pray, you will get the accolades from God, not man. He is absolutely faithful. Be sure prayer is at the top of your priority list of things to do.

Chapter 3
The Fall

In 1976, my brother and his girlfriend decided to go on a fun trip for the weekend at a popular ski resort. We said our good-byes as they left for their trip. Both of them were so excited. They arrived at the ski resort, and the unimaginable happened: while riding in the ski lift, his girlfriend frantically told him that the chair seemed to be broken. All of sudden, the chair began to sway backward and forward. His girlfriend passed out before they fell to the ground. They were ninety feet in the air. The news reporter said that my brother fell and bounced twenty-five feet down the canyon, and, amazingly, he landed on his two feet. It took a hundred rescuers to locate them. My brother was conscious, and the rescuer heard his cry. He and his girlfriend were airlifted in a helicopter to the hospital.

We received the telephone call from the hospital regarding this awful accident. It was on every news station. We immediately contacted all our family members, and we caravanned to the hospital. The ride was two hours long. My brother-in-law was the driver of our car, and he fell asleep while driving. I was in the back seat with my sister, and I felt the car spinning uncontrollably on the freeway. It was raining so hard. I woke up, and the car went over the freeway exit ramp. I thought the car was going to tip over because it was leaning on one side. We climbed out of a car window because it was the only way we could get out. But thank God, we got out safely.

It was a miracle that a police officer witnessed the accident and came to our rescue. We were shivering, and it was raining like cats and dogs. My brother-in-law, with the help of the officer, was able to get the car back on the road. God is a miracle worker. Can you imagine this happening while we were on our way to the hospital to check on my brother and his girlfriend, who had been in a terrible ski lift accident? We told the officer this story, and the officer informed us that he heard about it on the news. We told him that we were OK, and we proceeded to the hospital. I was a nervous wreck. I prayed all the way to the hospital for God to protect us. The weather was extremely bad.

We arrived at the hospital, and we whispered a prayer for my brother. It was terrible; his head was busted open, his pelvis was broken, his knee cap was fractured and sticking out of his leg, and he had internal bleeding. The doctors could not give him an anesthetic. Even from outside we could hear my brother's screams as the doctor drilled a hole in his knee and put a rod and pins in his leg. My God, it was done without anesthetic. It was the most horrific cry I have ever heard. His girlfriend's face was disfigured from the fall, and she was in a coma. The doctors said there was nothing they could do for his girlfriend. They said that my brother would never walk again, and that his girlfriend would be a vegetable for the rest of her life.

It was unbelievable what they had experienced. But my God is awesome. My brother told my mother, "Don't worry, I am going to walk. God is a miracle worker." One of the doctors told us he was an atheist, but he admitted that there must be a God, because God completely healed my brother. When you look at them now, it is unbelievable that they survived a ninety-foot fall. Several years after the accident, my brother's girlfriend gave birth to a child. This young man is now one of the greatest soul winners anointed and appointed by God. His testimony is electrifying. There is power in prayer. James 5:14–15 says, "Is any sick among you? let him call for the elders of the church; and let them pray over him, anointing him with oil in the name of the Lord: And the prayer of faith shall save the sick." It is irresistible what God can do for those who believe in the power of prayer.

Sometimes we fall from grace, but God is merciful if you will submit and yield yourself to Him. I love Jude 24: "Now unto him that is able to keep you from falling, and to present you faultless before the presence of his glory with exceeding joy."

On Friday, February 15, 2009, I received devastating news: my son was hospitalized. I remember it like it was yesterday. He was a healthy young man, and took very good care of his physical body. He was employed and educated. But he said his work and his mobile skills were off. He prayed, and he knew something was wrong. As a mom, I'm telling you, it is good to have the Lord on your side. He drove himself to the hospital, and immediately they kept him. He was unable to swallow, and when I got to the hospital, he had a feeding tube in him. I had to be strong because I didn't want him to panic. I prayed, and I could see that he was tense. The doctor said his nervous system was shutting down his immune system. They don't know what caused this rare affliction.

My son said that all he could think about was that he did not want to be confined to a wheelchair. But he could not walk on his own. For awhile, he could not swallow, which is the reason they had to put a tube in him. I prayed, and on the third day, God blessed us by allowing the tube to be removed, and he was able to swallow. As he got better, he was released from the hospital. The physical therapy for his recovery was not easy. My daughter moved in with him to help take care of him. Finally, after months of physical therapy and willpower, he was completely healed. God is a healer, regardless of the symptoms.

You might fall from grace, but God is immutable, which means he is unchangeable. When you are on your sick bed, He will remind you that He is God. All you have to do is say, "Yes, Lord, I will obey," and that is what my son said. He totally surrendered his will to God. I've learned not to let anyone stop you from God's divine plan for your life. Sometimes God needs to stop us in our tracks because we are too busy to listen. What I love about God is that He will give you enormous strength and might to stand against the evil forces and powers of darkness that come against you mentally, physically, and emotionally. Regardless of what you have experienced—it could be an unhealthy relationship, rebellious children, divorce, the loss of a loved one, dealing with difficult people, or financial difficulties—if you feel like you have fallen, get up by the grace of God. Let the affirmation of the scriptures be your daily power source. Jude 24 says that He is "able to keep you from falling," and Philippians 4:13 says, "I can do all things through Christ which strengtheneth me."

Chapter 4
Where Is God? The Fistfight

I was always the one who believed it is important to maintain your integrity in the midst of your storms. The difficulties, uncertainties, and despair of one's destiny sometimes makes you wonder if God is all-knowing. To be honest, I said, "Lord, why did this happen to me?" In my spirit, I felt isolated, abandoned, and alienated from the very presence of God. I believe God is eternal, and that His existence has no beginning and will have no ending. He always was, always is, and always will be, according to Genesis 1:1. The Bible clearly lets us know of His presence in Psalm 14:1: "The fool hath said in his heart, There is no God."

Maintaining my integrity was costly. I had to resist my emotions and abdicate my true feelings when I had a fistfight at the age of forty. I was taught that God is omniscient and that He knows all things. He knows all of the chaos that happens in this present world. So, why was it that I was not warned about the abuse coming to me? What came alive in my mind was Hebrews 12:1, which says, "Wherefore seeing we also are compassed about with so great a cloud of witnesses, let us lay aside every weight and the sin which doth so easily beset us, and let us run with patience the race that is set before us." In this Christian race, we're in preparation to enter life's conflicts with the assurance that God is able to bring us out. I had to understand that although I experienced this change of events, I could not keep iniquity in my heart, and I had to forgive those who tried to harm me.

It happened on a Wednesday evening. I was getting ready to attend Bible study when my brother's ex-girlfriend and a guy came into my home through the back door. It was safe to leave your doors open back in the day. I was shocked that these intruders came into my residence to harm me. I pleaded with the ex-girlfriend to please leave with the guy that was with her.

The ex-girlfriend went into a hysterical demonic rage and started using profanity. She grabbed me and started tearing my clothes and hitting me. I told her that I did not want to fight because I was saved. She said, "You act like you go with your brother."

I told her that this was not true. She was angry with my brother because he had ended their relationship. My brother resided with me at the time. He was not saved, and he sure didn't keep company with saints. My brother and I were always close, and we had a good relationship.

I kept pleading with her to please leave. She refused, and she continued to become more demonic. I continued to say, "I am saved, and I do not want to fight you." She ignored my pleas. My mom lived two doors down from me, and I reached for the phone to call for help. Immediately, she snatched the phone out of the wall.

"Oh, Lord," I prayed, and I kept pleading with her. She ignored me one again and told the guy, "Get the gun." He reached for his pocket, and instantaneously, with all my might, I went into a karate mode and kicked his hand.

Now I can laugh at the incident, and I say the Lord taught me how to do martial arts, karate, and kung fu. Whatever moves I made startled the young man, and he ran out of the house. I did not see him anymore, but the ex-girlfriend continued to battle with me. You could see the demonic expressions of Satan himself on this young lady. She was cursing and saying words I was not accustomed to hearing. I was doing all I could to protect my face from her blows. She was strong, and I needed all my strength to defend myself. I was praying, and I knew that if I did not defend myself, I was going to die. It was a vicious battle for survival.

Satan's desire is to abduct your integrity and your strong desire to be like Jesus. How could I be like Jesus and have a fistfight? It seemed like hours of battling with this demonic person. I was praying and doing all I could to keep her from killing me. She was going for blood. Finally, she got tired from the fight, and she left my residence. I felt faint from the fight. And I was so upset because my safe haven had been violated.

When she left my residence, she lied and told her family that my six sisters had jumped her. It was no more than fifteen minutes after the incident that God sent my uncle over, who is a Muslim, and whom I had not seen in about a year. He stopped by to use the bathroom. What an awesome God. He may not come when you want Him, but He's always on time. It's amazing how God can work in the midst of your storm. I was so shaken up, and I told my uncle I had just gotten into a fight. He was surprised. I explained to him that it was with my brother's ex-girlfriend, and that she had been angry because he'd ended their relationship.

While my uncle was in the bathroom, I looked out the window and fear gripped me. The ex-girlfriend had come back with two carloads of people. When my uncle came out of the bathroom, I frantically said, "Look, there are two carloads of people." Can you imagine if I had been home alone? I would not be alive to tell my story. These individuals had come with the intention to kill me.

By that time, my family arrived; my sisters and five brothers were on the scene. I opened the door to explain to the ex-girlfriend's mom what had really taken place, and the ex-girlfriend began to attack me with a knife. I have the scar to prove that she cut me. I got the knife away from her, and then her mom started hitting one of my sisters. My brothers and sisters were being attacked by the people who came along with her. The scene was like a war zone. I had never witnessed anything like that in our neighborhood.

We all were trying to protect ourselves. I kept screaming, "I am saved, and she came into my house and jumped me." I can't remember how many times I said, "I'm saved." What powerful words. The Holy Ghost began to move. I screamed out with a loud voice, "I'm saved." All of sudden, the people stopped and looked at me as if they had seen a ghost. It was miraculous! They began to get in their cars. When they left, my brothers confiscated eleven knives, and the tears began to stream down my face as I thought about the greatness of God. He was there in the fistfight, and He helped me win the physical battle.

Sometimes Christians think that walking with Christ means that you are exempt from the pressures of life. I'm reminded of the apostle Paul, who was beaten with rods and was stoned, and who had to endure great suffering. Yet we judge those who experience challenges in their lives. I'm not sure if we deliberately disconnect ourselves from them or if we are not aware that it is Satan using you to look down on your sister or brother. We have the tendency to treat others badly if they are not saved. From my personal experience, I was saved, sanctified, filled, and called into the ministry.

Yet it was difficult for me to keep my spiritual sanity. I remember that I was so embarrassed after that incident, and I heard the voice of God speak to me in a still, small voice and say, "My child, I love you, and I have chosen you. Many are going to see you and call you blessed." In my human mind, I was wondering how I could be blessed while I was being humiliated. The Holy Ghost took me to Isaiah 55:8: "For my thoughts are not your thoughts, neither are your ways my ways, saith the Lord."

I cried for two weeks because I had experienced what I felt was the worst battle of my spiritual sanity. It took me awhile to abdicate my feelings of hopelessness. Yes, I questioned my position as being a saintly woman of God. But I knew that God was there in the midst of my humanity. My human instincts were there to protect myself. Even though I had to fight to survive, I still called on the name of Jesus. What do you do if you fall victim to difficulties? Satan is an accuser of the brethren. He tells you that you are not saved. Satan tormented me day and night after the fight. I had many sleepless nights after my experience. It was hard for me to stay focused. I cried and cried, and just could not get over the fact that although I was forty years old, saved, sanctified, and filled with the Holy Ghost, I had had a fistfight.

Regardless of the negativity I experience, I prayed and asked God for forgiveness. I still had a strong desire to be like Jesus. I thought about how bridges have abatements, which is the support at the end of the arch. I leaned on Jesus because He is the bridge over troubled waters.

I thought about one of my favorite scriptures, which is the second chapter of Ezekiel. Ezekiel was commissioned, and the Spirit of God entered him and gave him strength to go to the children of Israel, who were a rebellious nation that rebelled against God. They and their fathers' had transgressed against God, and they were stiff-hearted people. I can identify with this chapter when my brother ex-girlfriend and her mother came against me, a child of God. One thing I love most about God is that He will give you enormous strength and might to stand against evil forces and the powers of darkness in order to declare the gospel to those who are lost.

In spite of all this chaos, good came out of this ordeal. The ex-girlfriend came over the next day, along with her mother, to apologize. This was my opportunity to witness to them. I shared the gospel of Jesus with them and prayed. I accepted their apology. When you are full of the Spirit of God, you understand the importance of forgiveness.

Every now and then, you ought to extend your love. You see, the opposite of anger is forgiveness. It is not easy to forgive those who harm you, but God will give you the grace to forgive, because His grace is sufficient. 2 Corinthians 12:9 says, "My grace is sufficient for thee: for my strength is made perfect in weakness."

Yes, an evangelist who was saved, sanctified, and filled with the Holy Ghost had a fistfight, and won the physical battle.

We find in Psalm 38 that David loves and is moved to compassion. You see, David recognized the brevity and vanity of life, and he knew how it is important to trust God. In verses 21 to 22, he speaks these words: "Forsake me not, O LORD: O my God, be not far from me. Make haste to help me, O LORD my salvation."

You see, God was there in the midst of my crisis. I no longer feel guilty. I've learned that if you want mental, spiritual, and emotional healing, you have to let go of the past. There will be no healing until there is repentance. I repented, even though it was not my fault, because I understood that the true power of freedom of the mind is when you have a change of heart. I can relate to those who are secretly trying to survive their personal struggles. I've been there, and I hope my experience will make a difference in your life or someone you know who is living in silent depression. I hope my testimony on paper will help you learn how to resolve unhealthy relationships, enjoy family and friends, and understand the importance of forgiveness. I'm here to encourage you that you can let go of the past of pain, anger, resentment, or bitterness. Let go and live!

Chapter 5
The Battle of Spiritual Sanity

When I married at the age of twenty-four, I believed my husband was God-sent. What attracted me to him was his sincere love of God. The man could preach, and when I dated him, he was kind, considerate, and gentle, and showered me with flowers and gifts. He was not stingy, and he liked nice things. He was a man who had goals. We dated and decided to marry. We had a beautiful wedding.

Now the question to ask is was he really the perfect match? I had mixed emotions regarding the chain events I had experienced during our courtship. I had no clue that he had a dark side to him. He was filled with jealousy far beyond the norm. Sometimes while you are in a relationship, you overlook the warning signs and feel that the person might change. A few months into my marriage, I was about to experience the worst battle for my spiritual sanity. In the age in which I married, you were taught to stay in your marriage. It did not matter if you were being abused mentally, physically, or verbally. Those old mothers said, "You stay and pray." The truth of the matter is that I did not see the signs of jealousy; when someone is showering you with a lot of gifts, you are blinded. I'm not saying that you should not receive gifts, but sometimes it becomes exorbitant to the point where you are only concerned about what you are receiving from the other person.

I did not have a clue that I was going to be a victim of domestic violence. Unfortunately, my prince charming began to physically abuse me. I could not understand how a man of the gospel could be so hateful. As I matured in the Lord, I realized that people are human and are not perfect. I'm not saying it's OK to accept abuse from anyone; what I am saying is that just because a person, male or female, can quote scriptures does not mean that they are following the principles of Christian living.

I loved to beat the tambourine because I was not blessed to sing. I was a member of the church choir and was a good tambourine player; it was my personal way of worship. One particular Sunday, the service was high and I was enjoying playing the tambourine to an upbeat song. I was having a good time. Once you are in a relationship, you learn how to communicate with your eyes or hand gestures. I noticed that my husband was trying to get my attention. He asked me to step outside. I had no clue as to what he wanted. I innocently went outside, and to my surprise, he slapped me in my face so hard. He said that I was shaking my behind. What was I to do? Should I tell the pastor? I was so shocked! I went back in the church as if nothing had happened. My face hurt so badly. He went back in the church and sat in the pulpit. He had no remorse, and I was so afraid to go home after service.

This was the beginning of my battle to keep my spiritual sanity. He argued in a rage of anger all the way home. I was so hurt, but I was too afraid to respond. I tried to avoid any confrontation that would escalate the problem. My mom taught me how to pray by me watching her life experiences. I prayed for God to give me strength. Can you imagine waiting on the Lord and all of a sudden the person you married does not love you anymore? You thought you were in the perfect will of God, but you are in an abusive relationship. You don't feel comfortable to share the abuse with anyone because you are a preacher's wife.

Lord, have mercy. The man I married was abusive, and I had to listen to him when he preached. Oh, the saints praised him for the dynamic word he preached. It was very difficult to sit and listen to a person who preached but lived another way behind closed doors. I wanted to stand up in the church and say, "You are a hypocrite." One thing I learned is that the scripture is true that gifts and calling are without repentance.

40

I definitely understand the role of a preacher's wife wears a mask, and how many preachers' wives are silent. M a deep secret, and they cannot reveal to anyone what they are expe- riencing. Through my experience, Scripture came alive. His Word will sustain you in the midst of the storm. Isaiah 43:2 is my favorite scripture: "When thou passest through the waters, I will be with thee; and through the rivers, they shall not overflow thee: when thou wal- kest through the fire, thou shalt not be burned; neither shall the flame kindle upon thee."

I believe the waters are your affliction. The *Webster Dictionary* defines *affliction* as grief or the distress of the body and mind. Sometimes our lives are full of troubles and despair, and we uncon- sciously allow our thought patterns to divert us from enjoying a life that will lead to our personal growth. God will give you faith to pass through your waters. My definition of faith was given to me by God several years ago: faith is living in perplexity and knowing that God will make a way for you to escape, which simply means that God will help you bear it.

I'm reminded of 1 Corinthians 10:13, "There hath no temptation taken you but such as is common to man: but God is faithful, who will not suffer you to be tempted above that ye are able; but will with the temptation also make a way to escape, that ye may be able to bear it."

When I experienced mental, emotional and physical abuse I did not share it with anyone. I was employed at my church as Pastors personal secretary and church secretary and remain silent. I was so ashamed. When you are in an abusive relationship you begin to blame oneself. Abuse is a life- changing episode of your emotions being shattered. I've learned that your brain has a mechanism to shut down to protect our mental state. When a person has an addiction they use drugs or alcohol to medicate their pain. We as Christians have the tendency to isolate ourselves and Satan deals with our thought pro- cess. In my marriage, I thought, *Am I satisfying him sexually? Are my meals good? Am I a good mother to my children?* I did the best I could to adjust to his physical, mental, and emotional needs. But I was never good enough. What did he really want from me? What do you do when you just don't understand? My answer is to rely on the Word of God. Now I understand Isaiah 26:3, "Thou wilt keep him in perfect peace, whose mind is stayed on thee: because he trusteth in thee." Many times I spoke these words. If it had not been for the Lord at my side, I would have been in a mental institution.

I was overwhelmed with sadness and despair because I was a victim of domestic violence. During that era, you did not talk about abuse. The only comfort I had was with the Lord. One morning I woke up early, around 2:00 a.m. I began to talk to the Lord, and I asked him a simple question: "Why do I have to suffer?"

Well, God answered me and said, "Do you remember the story of Job?" God said that it is a blessing to be chosen by Him to suffer, and that I did not need to be ashamed. He said, "Many will look upon you and call you blessed."

I did not quite understand what God was saying, because I was just in my early twenties. Now as a matured Christian, it is amazing to see how God believed in me. He had enough confidence in me that He knew no matter what I encountered, I would trust Him.

I still had some storms to ride. One of the scariest things was the fact that I didn't know what would trigger his emotions. One particular Sunday morning, I notice a pot of boiling water on the stove. I frantically ran out of the house and could hear him calling for me. His mom lived across the street, and she had no clue as to what I was experiencing. I calmed myself down and acted as if nothing was wrong. I mastered the technique of acting like everything was OK. He had no clue as to my whereabouts. I'm not sure the water was boiling for me, but it was the fear that I lived in. I was not taking any chances. I stayed for awhile, and went home when he left the residence. When he returned home, he came back with six dresses he'd purchased for me. The dresses were beautiful, but I still was unhappy.

He asked, "Where did you go?"

I replied, "Over to your mom's house."

For some reason, even after his abuse, he believed things made me happy. But no matter how he tried to make me happy with material things, I still had a void in my life. Yes, I drove a silver Cadillac Seville. You can have houses, money, and cars, but if you do not have a relationship with God, there is emptiness in your life. Luke 12:15 says, "Take heed, and beware of covetousness: for a man's life consisteth not in the abundance of the things which he possesseth."

Satan is our enemy, and it is his job to cause you to deviate from God's divine will for your life. Because I enjoyed a nice house, a Cadillac Seville, and clothes, I became victimized in my own home. My life was like a vacuum. I continue to remain a victim of abuse.

It's amazing how the victim protects the batterer. As a preacher's wife, who could I talk to? He was popular, and it was possible that the church members would not believe me. I knew that if I told my five brothers, who were not saved, it would cause a chain of explosive episodes of revenge.

I became a professional pretender because I knew if I resisted his actions, he would talk to me negatively all night long, and if I dozed off, I would get slapped hard in the face. I went through mental and verbal abuse for long periods in the morning. The abuse might start at 2:00 a.m., and he would continue to antagonize me till 6:00 a.m., when I had to get ready to report to work the following day.

When I arrived at work, I would be so tired, and it was only the grace of God that kept me going. No one at work knew what I was going through at home. I always maintained a professional and pleasant attitude. The abuse escalated until he would drop me off at work, and the security guard would say good morning. When my husband would pick me up from work, the interrogation would start. "I saw you talking to the security guard." He would hit me over and over. I prayed, prayed, prayed. Finally, he would stop, and I would fall asleep.

How do you survive in adversity? Can you imagine getting hit all night long? I got to the point in my mind where I just had to get over it, accept it, and move on. What happens when you go into a defense mode of denial? Listen to the words, get over it, accept it, and move on. How can you get over being beaten all night? You feel that you have no choice but to accept this abuse, and you think that maybe you are to blame.

You do everything to keep your spiritual sanity. You avoid arguing while he is in a demonic rage. Domestic violence is power and controlling. The batterer feels that he has the right to dominate you. My ex-husband used material things to keep control of me. I wanted my own independence, and I wanted to pursue a career in criminal justice to become a probation officer. I decided to enroll in Compton College to study criminal justice. I thought this was my opportunity to get away from the norm of my controlling husband. I was shocked to see that my ex-husband had enrolled in the same class without telling me. He had the nerve to arrive late in class and to ask me to sit by him. I was so humiliated to the point that I dropped out of the class.

In that era, you did not talk about needing a marriage counselor. All we heard was to pray and to not divorce your husband under any circumstances. I was so miserable, and to be honest, I began to have suicidal thoughts. I was a stressed out woman, and my life was in disarray. The most difficult aspect was being married to a preacher who had demonic characteristics, and who refused to allow the Holy Spirit to guide his family in love. I don't believe God makes mistake. Sometimes I wonder if I saw the signs. What are the signs? When a person gives you so many nice gifts in the earlier part of your relationship, it could be an indication that he or she is hiding their real selves. I was showered with so many gifts that I did not see the signs of jealousy. I believe so many women are trapped in a web of deceit by being selfish. We just want to be showered with stuff, and we lose focus of who we are. It reminds me of Luke 12:15, which says that man's life consists not in the abundance of things which he possesses. It seems to be a redundant statement, but it is true: we value our worth with things.

I vividly remember it as if it was yesterday. As newlyweds, our first residence was a one-bedroom apartment. There was one way in and one way out. My mom had not heard from me, and she was concerned. She came by the house, and I could not let her in because my ex-husband had locked me in the house. He decided that I was not going to work, and he boarded up the windows so that I could not escape. I was employed at Security Pacific National Bank, which was located on Fifth Main Street in Los Angeles. My job was downtown, adjacent to Skid Row. He allowed me to call my job to inform my supervisor that I was sick. I was so embarrassed and humiliated because I had to converse with mom through the mail slot. I was traumatized because I was not allowed to visit my family. There were days when I cannot tell you how I got dressed. I kept my problems in the house.

One Sunday morning after worship service, we were driving home, and my ex-husband was arguing with me while driving at a high speed on the 710 freeway. I really don't know what caused the chain of events. But I was so scared because he was acting like he wanted to kill us. Before I knew it, I reached to open the door to jump out of the car. But I praise God for preventing me from committing suicide, because the car door was locked. My ex-husband gave me a look and then was silent. It shocked him that I was about to commit suicide.

The angels of God were encamped around me and helped me battle my spiritual sanity. We serve an awesome God who will protect you and help you win the warfare of defeat.

Later, my ex-husband purchased a beautiful home for us. I was young in the '70s, driving a silver Cadillac Seville, and I had plenty of clothes, shoes, and hats. Although I had the finest of things, my life was in disarray because I was married to a man who had demonic characteristics.

I was called into ministry at the age of eighteen years old, and the odds were against women preachers. I remember how the brethren ostracized women in the ministry. I had just graduated from high school. Satan tried to stop me from completing God's divine plan for my life. God's purpose was for me to minister to hurting people. My ministry was to bring spiritual awareness to those who were in bondage and felt they could not break loose from the emotions of anxiety, loneliness, depression, anger, guilt, rejection, spousal abuse, interpersonal relationships, substance abuse, and homosexuality, even though my own personal experiences were hard. I knew that one day, if I waited on my ministry, God was going to bring me deliverance. I was to help those hurting people realize that to live in denial is an act of Satan to keep them in bondage.

In my early twenties, I had one of the greatest opportunities of a lifetime: to travel with a well-known evangelist. She heard me speak, and she told me that I reminded her of herself when she was my age. She asked if I wanted to travel with her. I was afraid to leave the nest because of my strong ties with my family. How many times have I refused to take an opportunity offered to me? It was my own insecurities that caused me to refuse to leave the nest. I cannot blame my family, because the choice was mine. In spite of my personal experience, I could feel God in the atmosphere, and I was full of excitement that God was going to bring me out victoriously. Sometimes in your life, you need to break away from your family, even though you love them. My mom, who was spiritual, was totally for me travelling with the well-known evangelist. I was so fearful and could not go, because I lacked spiritual maturity. When I started experiencing personal attacks by Satan, I thought if I would have obeyed God and travelled with the evangelist, I would have avoided these heartaches.

I've learned to be happy in spite of the storms of life. To live a life of joy comes from within you. You have to dig deep in your soul and believe what the Bible says. I kept quoting Isaiah 26:3 over and over: "Thou wilt keep him in perfect peace, whose mind is stayed on thee." Believe it or not, it works.

I was sharing with my son, who is thirty-four years old, and we began to discuss my life story of abuse. He said, "Momma, I remember the abuse. I was ten years old, and I saw you in a physical altercation, and I was so afraid." He told me how he and my oldest daughter would hide baseball bats behind the coach to come to my defense. He reminded me how he came to my rescue to help defend me, and how my ex-husband hit him on his neck. He was so afraid. He said that people do not know how abuse impacts children. He constantly lived in fear, and it caused him to become antisocial. He understood how women were taught that the man was the head of the household, and that I was not allowed to speak up. He said that the one thing about me was that I was not afraid to react to my abuse; when my husband hit me, I fought back. My son said I was not weak, and how he admired the fact that I did not become weak and irresponsible. I continued to raise my family, and I took them roller-skating, to movies, to dinner, and to church. I tried to raise my children like my mom raised me: with love and discipline. Church and family were important to me. My son is thirty-four years old; in spite of his experiences with seeing what spousal abuse is all about, he continued his education and received his master's in 2003, and now he is in his PhD program. I did not take out my frustration on my children. I focused my energy into making my children happy.

Although my son was quiet, he turned out to be a great guy, and his two sisters are great women.

My son's reenactment of my abuse reminds me of my next experience of abuse. This particular day, I reacted to the abuse. To be honest, I spoke to the Lord and said, "Your blood is not working; excuse me, Jesus, but tonight it is on." Well, my actions may not have been biblical, but I refused to turn the other cheek. I balled up my fist and hit him back.

We fought for a long period of time. I left the home and called my sister from the pay phone to pick me up. She came and said, "If he jumps on you, I am going to help you." Lord, I was shocked when I opened the door to pick up my belongings and found that he had them packed neatly in boxes. He was standing over them with a rifle. I was shaken because I did not know that he had a rifle. All I could think of was that he could have killed me in my sleep. The last words he spoke to me were, "Take only the boxes." When my sister saw the rifle, she ran out of the house and left me. I was a nervous wreck, and I left with only the items in the boxes. Well, the question that is often asked is why I stayed. First of all, I was embarrassed; my own insecurities and pride allowed me to self-blame, and I believed that the failed marriage was my fault. All those mixed emotions continue to torment me. I still have to believe that God has healed my feelings of rejection, and for me to value myself as worthy is a constant battle.

Yes, I have experienced pains of sadness, depression, and anxiety, but in the midst of my storm, I continue to be active in my local church. I remember the black eyes, and how I learned how to wear makeup to cover them. In our church, we were not allowed to wear makeup. But I did not care about this church rule. I was trying to survive and keep my spiritual sanity. I wanted to look good, and I learned how to be a professional pretender. Somehow, I was protecting my abuser. What would it look like for a preacher to be beating his wife, and what would the church think? Wow, this is deep. How many preachers' wives live in silence, crying? Until you experience it, don't be judgmental. We have used our survival skills, and we ride out those thoughts of defeat and move on. I'll never forget the words spoken to me by my former pastor ten years ago. He said, "God has a call on your life, and don't let anything cause you to deviate from His will. Many souls are standing in the balance. Seek God that He will reveal His perfect will for your life, and turn everything else loose: pride, self-will, and personal desire. Let God have His way with you; that's the only way you'll ever be happy."

Those words have carried me through every battle; regardless of the problem, I still hold on to hope. God will answer my prayers and help me. Satan knows how to give you a low blow, and when you feel ease, here comes another attack.

In order to survive Satan's attacks, I've learned to ride them out. I start talking to myself and saying, "I know it is difficult, but with the help of God, I will make it." Sometimes it is difficult to hear people's advice. How do you "let go and let God"? It's simple: believe His word. The fear you experience is temporary. The Bible teaches that as we become more like Jesus, our life will show the fruits of the spirit, which include patience, kindness, and self-control. To keep your spiritual sanity, you have to tune in with your subconscious mind; don't allow your thought patterns to deviate you from enjoying a life that will lead to your spiritual growth.

I am going to keep it real; yes, there was sex, but no intimacy. When it came to lovemaking, I just could not bring myself to even kiss my husband, because I was emotionally detached because of all the abuse. Don't get me wrong; I know from a scale of one to ten, I consider myself a great kisser. But I hated when he touched me, and I mastered the right moves and words to make him think I was enjoying him sexually. I was emotionally divorced from him, and I used to feel guilty because I thought God was going to punish me for pretending.

Yes, I was familiar with 1 Corinthians 7:4–5: "The wife hath not power of her own body, but the husband: and likewise also the husband hath not power of his own body, but the wife. Defraud ye not one the other, except it be with consent for a time, that ye may give yourselves to fasting and prayer; and come together again, that Satan tempt you not for your incontinency." What the scripture is saying is the wife and the husband has the right to satisfy the needs of the other. But I did not enjoy the sex, because of his abuse. He was so controlling, I only had sex to keep my spiritual sanity. How many preachers' wives are experiencing this same problem of being forced to have sex? Sex is beautiful expression of love created by God. Let me say, when you are being abused the desire to have sex is the farthest thing from your mind. You are ashamed to have sex. You know that, emotionally, you are disconnected. But to avoid upsetting your abusive husband, you cooperate. You learn how to resurrect your mental and spiritual state by believing that God will heal your broken heart.

My life experiences of disappointment, despair, anger, and betrayal of trust crushed me and hurt my feelings. In the battle of my mind, I had to pray, pray, pray that God would help me keep my sanity. I learned to praise God, and that He would deliver my soul from the lowest pit of hell. God is not like man; we have the tendency to judge one another, but according to Psalm 86:15, God is full of compassion and grace; He is longsuffering and has plenty of mercy. He will give you strength. I praise God that I'm not bitter and that I continue to move forward in the beauty of holiness. I don't struggle with low self-esteem and feelings of inferiority and worthlessness. I understand who God is and the awesome power He can provide in my life.

Thanks to God, I won the battle of spiritual sanity according to 2 Timothy 1:7: "For God hath not given us the spirit of fear; but of power, and of love, and of a sound mind."

Chapter 6
Mommy, You Are Heaven-Sent

The life of my mom is a true legacy of a widow who did not stop living. My mom lived by four principles; I call them the formula of life. Her formula is simple: to love God, people, family, and your church. Most people feel that only material things make you happy. If this was the case, why do we have a high rate of suicide for those who are successful financially? I understand why, and the Bible clearly states it in Luke 12:15, "Take heed, and beware of covetousness: for a man's life consisteth not in the abundance of things which he possesseth." The problem is that we have a yearning and aspiration for things, and we become selfish. My mom taught us early in life to be sure that you put God first, and that He will give you the desires of your heart.

My mother was affectionately called Mommy. She was born on March 17, 1934, in Pawhuska, Oklahoma, and moved to California when she was three years old. She married her high school sweetheart, Roman, and gave birth to twelve children (seven girls and five boys). She accepted the Lord into her life in 1959. She became a foster mom and raised eleven foster children. Mom did not show any difference between them and her own children. I remember a time when her friend, who was also a foster parent, bragged on how she shopped at the Goodwill stores for her foster kids. Mom thought it was a disgrace, and she refused to shop at the Goodwill store. Those kids wore name-brand clothes and shoes.

She was a disciplinarian, and made sure you were well dressed before you left the house. I remember Mom talking to all of my nieces and telling them, "Do not go out of the house looking messy." You would be in big trouble if you had rollers in your hair and not combed going out in public.

Our family tradition is to attend church every Sunday, and to have Tuesday-night prayer with our children. There is one more family tradition Mom started: the celebration of the fortieth birthday of each one of her children. Because Mom gave us love and security as children, we were able to develop physically, emotionally, and spiritually in spite of some hardships we experienced in our early childhood and teen years.

She enjoyed her life, and she most importantly loved her family, especially when we got together for recreation and fun activities. She loved to go to Disneyland, Knott's Berry Farm, Universal Studios, movies, the park, the Ice Capades, the zoo, Chuck E. Cheese's, and Discovery Zone with the children. When the children sometimes showed anger, disappointment, or sadness, Mom encouraged them to pray.

My mom knew how to guard her emotions, and when Dad died, her grieving process was smooth; she did not go into a depression. She remained faithful to the church for over thirty years. My mom was a member of an organization called the Supreme Ladies Charity Foundation, where she was crowned queen of the foundation for three consecutive years. She was also an active member of another organization, for which she was blessed to travel the world, visiting Jamaica, Hawaii, Switzerland, Italy, Paris, and the Holy Land, where she was baptized in the Jordan River. She went to the Grand Canyon and Canada, and to my surprise, she had an adventurous flight on a helicopter. She is a great example for widows who find it difficult to live without their spouse. She loved her family, and all of her daughters, sisters-in-law, and sisters attended God's Woman conferences for over fifteen years together. We had a great time.

Mommy was a prayer warrior. She had a great sense of humor, and was a woman of perseverance and deep commitment to God, family, and the community. She was not self-righteous.

On July 22, 2008, Mommy received her heavenly crown. I was amazed at the hundreds of people who came to my mom's house during her illness. My mom never was in the hospital, with the exception of giving birth to her twelve children. In March 2008, we got the devastating news that Mom had cervical cancer. We sat in the doctor's office, looking at my mom and listening to her response. I will never forget the words of the doctor: he informed us that she had between six months and one year to live. We were in shock.

My mom asked the doctor, "If I have surgery, will it prolong my life?" The doctor said no, and then my mom asked, "If I receive chemo, will it prolong my life?" and he said no again! My sister and I looked at one another with disbelief. I did not quite understand; here was a lady who had never been in the hospital or been sick.

My mom responded with, "Well, I'm not doing chemo or surgery."

The doctor said, "I have seen many patients who have sat in your place, and not one accepted the reality that they are going to die."

My mother responded by saying, "God has only promised me three scores and ten. He has blessed me with three scores and ten."

The death of my mom made me realize that death is a process. It was amazing to see how my mom never lost consciousness; she knew everyone who visited her. Hundreds of people came to my mom's home during her illness. To see the love of the neighbors, community, friends, church, and family was overwhelming. We receive so many flowers, cards, and monetary gifts; it was amazing. My mom was not a missionary, dignitary, or official. She was a humble woman who loved God. The Bible says that your works will speak for you. I saw it come alive during my mom's illness.

During my mom's sickness, I experienced the grace of God. My mom became very ill on a Monday, and she was rushed to the hospital; this was the first time she experienced severe pain. She began to cry, and in loud voice, she said, "God, why am I suffering like this? You promised me that I shall live and not die. You are a good God. Lord, thy will be done." Mom started speaking in her heavenly language. It was too much to hear my mom cry in anguish, and my sisters and I ran out of the room. No one can ever tell me that God does not exist. I witnessed the mighty hand of God during her anguish, and how she was able to calm down. She prayed the pain off her. She began to rest peacefully, and she never experienced this pain again.

On Tuesday, I spent the night at the hospital with her. My mom experienced an anxiety attack in the early-morning hours around 2:00

a.m., and she was restless. I began to pray, and she prayed and became calm. Mom said she wanted to go home and that her stay at the hospital would be short, only two days. Mom did not show any fear in the process. She seemed to enjoy her family.

I believe we all were in denial and really did not believe Mom was going to die. I did not know that hospice nurse care is the final stage of death. We had twenty-four-hour care at home. So in my mind, I felt that we were just giving Mom the greatest care. I occasionally would talk to the hospice nurse and ask if Mom was in pain. She said, "No! Look at your mom; by now, she should be screaming and hollering because the cancer is at stage four." My mom was resting peacefully. The nurse told me that Mom would leave this life fast.

It was amazing; Mommy knew every person by name who came to visit her. She never complained, and she still joined us in the Tuesday-night family prayer. For the Tuesday prayer meeting in the month of May, she called a meeting with all twelve children. She told us we had better not fuss or argue and embarrass her. We needed to continue to love one another, and she told the younger family members to go to college and to do well in school. She also said, "Do not be angry with God."

The following week, I received a telephone call at 2:00 a.m. from my sister, who said to get to Mom's house right away. My mom was not feeling well; she didn't say much, and her voice was shallow. She said to my baby brother, "You have to be strong." We started praying and praising God as we waited for the transition to her new life. The hospice nurse said, "Your mom is about to take her last breath." We were doing alright until she took her last breath; then we all started crying. I cried until my nose started bleeding, and they had to calm me down or I would have had to be rushed to the hospital. I just could not believe that my precious mother was gone. She was the rock of the family, the glue that kept us together.

The planning of the funeral was awesome. Her pastor came to help us with the final arrangements. She loved her pastor and first lady. I was blessed to have my pastor and the support of my church family. It helped me in the grieving process. When the family viewed the body, she was so beautiful in her gold suit and a crown on her head that none of us cried. She looked like an angel. We were so touched when we saw the thirty flower arrangements that had been delivered to the funeral home.

The day of the funeral was awesome. I never saw anything like it. My sister and nieces used their decorative creativity; they had a red carpet at the entry of the church, and it was surrounded with red roses and two pillars with her fabulous hats on them. Inside the two pillars were gold drapes. My son had pictures of family members who had earned their bachelor's, master's, and juris doctorate degrees, and the forty-eight grandchildren who had graduated from school. She was so proud of her family accomplishments.

Over two thousand people attended Mom's funeral. It was amazing to see so many people come from far and near. My husband, Samuel, did an excellent job as the officiant of her homegoing celebration of life. I am so grateful for all those who gave their time, monetary gifts, cards, food, and floral arrangements. A special thank you goes to K.C., who was a blessing to our family. He was responsible for the party van, which the grandchildren rode within in style, and his monetary gift. We love Brother K.C.

In the midst of this loss, I saw the greatness of God, and how Mom accepted the will of God without complaining. What an awesome woman of God. When death knocks on my door, I truly understand the scripture that says we are promise three score years and ten, and that by reason of strength, there may be fourscore years (Psalm 90:10). The normal life God promises is seventy years. My mom's experience lets me know that we better live righteously, because one day we are going to cross over to eternal death or life.

I was at peace at my mom's homegoing, and I believe the scripture that says to be absent from the body is to be at rest with the Lord (II Corinthians 5:8). I rejoiced during my mom's homegoing because I had no guilty feelings or shame, because I honored my mom like the Bible said.

Mom's homegoing became a witnessing tool for me to share the love of God in the beauty of His holiness. I continue to live the four principles of life: love God, family, church, and people. These are the keys to successful living. Thank you, Mom; you are heaven-sent.

Chapter 7
Refuse to Feel Guilty
Because of Haters

I n the court system, there is a prosecutor and a defense attorney. The role of the prosecutor is to present evidence that you are guilty, and the defense is to show you are innocent of the crime you are charged with. In this life, Satan is the prosecutor, and he tries to intimidate you with his fiery darts. He uses people to distract you from your purpose. Jesus is the defense attorney, and because of the blood of Jesus, He is our resurrected power. The resurrection power will help you overcome all obstacles that negatively impact your life. He will help you overcome feelings of not fitting in, of self-pity, of resentment, and of the desire to pull others into conflicts. The Bible says in Psalm 34:18, "The Lord is nigh unto them that are of a broken heart; and saveth such as be of a contrite spirit." The word *contrite* means "shortcomings."

I can only speak what I have experienced; my purpose of writing this book is not to bash the church, because I love the church. I want this book to encourage someone who is dressed up in fancy hats, designer shoes, and clothes, but who is emotionally isolated and suffering from depression, and who learned survival skills by being emotionally isolated or disconnected while sitting in church. We know how to wear a mask; I did it for years until I just got sick and tired. What I have written is not popular. I know there are thousands of self-help books. I say to all those who think they know how a

ls, until you walk in their shoes, don't judge. Also, I'd like
I hear a lot of people who give their opinion about topics
tnat tney think they are experts on. Most women or men who are
married don't have a clue, so they only quote scriptures. You cannot
even imagine how a person who is a victim of abuse feels mentally,
emotionally, and physically. If you have never experienced your mate
being abusive, then you cannot understand. Based on my experience, only God can direct you as to when the relationship should be
terminated. I understand that Paul speaks about not dissolving your
marriage. I was persecuted by my church family; they overlooked
me and tried to condemn me. My best girlfriends turned their backs
and isolated me from their group. This church abuse was sometimes
unbearable. But when you know your purpose, the haters will not
determine your destiny. I survived through prayer and reading God's
Word. One of my favorite scripture is Isaiah 43:25: "I, even I, am he
that blotteth out thy transgressions for mine own sake, and will not
remember thy sins." This scripture will help you overcome feeling
that you are not good enough. Your past is only a tool to help you
get to the next level of becoming a role model to empower others to
move beyond adversities and to allow their inner spirit to blossom.

The haters can't understand how you can walk with your head
up and continue to praise God in the midst of your storms. Trust me;
people are aware of your experiences, but they might never address
them, because they are afraid they will not be in the class of the
so-called professional pretenders in the church. Yes, I experienced
so many hurts in the church, but I knew the Word, and the Bible is
clear that we should not be selfish. Matthew 22:39 says, "And the
second is like unto it, Thou shalt love thy neighbor as thyself." To
love your neighbor is an indication that you love God and that you
are His disciple. John 13:35 says, "By this shall all men know that
ye are my disciples, if ye have love one to another."

Although I was being persecuted, I learned not to listen to people
who made you feel irrelevant. When I was younger in the ministry, I
had a difficult time dismissing negative feelings toward them because
their actions that they had deliberately tried to hurt me. My
very supportive, and I was scheduled to preach Sunday eve-
vited thirty family members to hear me, but as I sat waiting

to minister, the coordinator called on someone else to preach. I was crushed. I was overwhelmed with hurt, but I managed to hold back the tears. I refused to let my haters see me cry. I actually enjoyed the speaker; it was not her fault. Only God is the master of your destiny, and He has the blueprint. The pastor of this particular church knew by the attendance of my family that I was supposed to be the scheduled speaker. The pastor sent me a note that said I would be speaking the following Sunday. We had a broadcast during this time, and I had no idea that mine was the last radio broadcast. God blessed me to speak, and radio listeners asked for copies of my tape.

We know there are haters in families and workplaces, and unfortunately they are in the church too. When you experience church abuse, it is mind-boggling. When we were young, we were treated differently because my mom had twelve children. My mom had a way of letting everyone know that she was proud to be a mom. When I got older, I realized she was skillful in dealing with all the haters in the church.

When we were treated differently, Mom put us in the fund raiser at the church, and we were competitive and came in first place. We won basically all of the fund raisers. She taught us at an early age not to be intimidated by anyone. There was one fund raiser where my twin sisters were involved. They raised lots of money. One of the rules was that the money had to be turned in at a certain time—no exceptions. My sister adhered to the rule and turned their money in by the deadline. One of the parents whose daughter was also competing found out how much money was turned in by my sisters, and they added an additional fifty dollars to their daughter's amount. One of the deacons collecting the money informed us of this. This action caused my sister to lose the competition. They cried for days. There were cheaters in the church, and it crushed my twin sisters because they had worked so hard. Well, it was like there was a code of silences to keep your mouth shut and not deal with the issue. I recognize that people in the church have a difficult time resolving conflicts. Once you hurt a teenager in the church, it is hard for some to recover. It was very sad emotionally for my sisters, and the parent was a missionary. Mom said, "Let it go. God will fix it, and He is going to bless you, because what you've done was unto the Lord."

Do you think teenagers understand this saying? Absolutely not. My sisters were hurt for a long time.

One day, a faithful church lady asked my sister Donna, "How do you all eat, and do you eat beans every day?"

Donna was outspoken, and she said, "We eat just like you eat."

My mom used to sit down and talk to me about what she had to go through with people in the church. My mom's response was just to pray for them. Well, we were young and angry, and did not understand. We were not disrespectful, but we said that we would never work in the church again. Now, I understand what Scripture means when it addresses strife. Strife is a prolonged struggle for power. Some people in the church will do anything to have power. I love Galatians 6:9, "And let us not be weary in well doing: for in due season we shall reap, if we faint not." I believe that you will experience a spiritual harvest if you faint not.

When we were young, we didn't know how to deal with the conflicts in the church. We learned at an early age that we would not resolve every conflict. We had to practice walking in the Spirit and not envying others. It happens, because we are still human, and no matter how much we are like Jesus, we still have a tendency to be unfair. If you are a perpetrator of unfairness, there is still forgiveness for you. Psalm 130:4 says, "But there is forgiveness with thee, that thou mayest be feared," and Ephesians 4:32 says, "And be ye kind one to another, tenderhearted, forgiving one another, even as God for Christ's sake hath forgiven you." Unfortunately, some will go to their grave without asking for forgiveness. We are not accountable for anyone but ourselves. My choice is to forgive, to continue to walk His light, and to have fellowship with my brothers and sisters.

My survival came from my persistent attitude. I have always been persistent in my service for God. It is not my fault if I have not been given the opportunity. Many people in the church seek prestige and are prejudiced, feeling they have precedent over you because they have their college degree, but the truth of the matter is that they don't have people skills when it comes to reaching those who need salvation. I am not confused regarding my purpose. God called me to be a soul winner. It is difficult working with difficult people in the workplace, in the church, or in families. They key to surviving this serious test is to have good self-esteem. It is important feel good about one-self, because those around you will try to make you a victim of their insecurities. I have had my share of haters, and I refuse to feel guilty because of who I am.

Sometimes people will attack your integrity. I knew who I belonged to, and I was able to pray and walk with my head up because I knew Christ had my back. If I tell you it never bothered me, I would not be truthful. I used to cry so hard until I thought I was about to lose my mind. One day, I fell on floor in the hallway and started screaming and kicking. I was overwhelmed with hurt. If my children saw me, they would have called the paramedics and had me admitted to the hospital. Can you imagine a forty-year-old woman on the floor, kicking and screaming? I was full of despair.

I told God, "I cannot take the pressures of life. Why do I have to suffer?" I had gone through so much, and I started to feel ashamed.

But God spoke to me and said, "I chose you to suffer, and it is a blessing to be chosen. I trust that you will not leave me." He reminded me of when Job was personally challenged by Satan, Job 1:6–12:

> Now there was a day when the sons of God came to present themselves before the LORD, and Satan came also among them. And the LORD said unto Satan, Whence comest thou? Then Satan answered the LORD, and said, From going to and fro in the earth, and from walking up and down in it. And the LORD said unto Satan, Hast thou considered my servant Job, that there is none like him in the earth, a perfect and upright man, one that feareth God, and escheweth evil? Then Satan answered the LORD, and said, Doth Job fear God for nought? Hast not thou made an hedge about him, and about his house, and about all that he hath on every side? Thou hast blessed the work of his hands, and his substance is increased in the land. But put forth thine hand now, and touch all that he hath, and he will curse thee to thy face. And the LORD said unto Satan, Behold, all that he hath is in thy power; only

upon himself put forth thine hand. So Satan went forth
from the presence of the LORD.

I learned reversed psychology on the haters in my workplace. I
refused to stay home and give them my time. I reported to work every
day. I knew it was all a matter of time before the individuals would
stress themselves out. I believe the Bible when it said, "Touch not my
anointed" (1 Chronicles 16:22). God will take care of the haters. You
need not worry, and do not allow Satan to make you feel inadequate
and have no self-worth. The devil is a liar. You are created in God's
image, and are wonderfully made.

I am a firm believer of 1 Corinthians 15:58: "Therefore, my
beloved brethren, be ye steadfast, unmovable, always abounding in
the work of the Lord, forasmuch as ye know that your labor is not
in vain in the Lord." This scripture sustained me in the midst of my
emotional turbulence. I can attest to my strong belief in God that
I have endured the greatest test of not only being in ministry, but
being a preacher's wife. This is why it is no longer difficult for me
to express my feelings as I disclose the many challenges I've faced.
I hope I am helping someone. It is a great price to be anointed by
God. I know some may say it doesn't cost you anything because He
paid it all on Calvary. Yes, He did, but you must remember Matthew
16:24: "If any man will come after me, let him deny himself, and take
up his cross, and follow me." The cross represents sacrifices. It cost
you to be saved, appointed, and anointed. Satan is out to wipe you
out. It is important for you to understand that we all are in a battle
to keep our sanity.

In particular, Satan's weapon is to discourage you and to make
you feel as though God is not concerned about your feelings. There
was a period in my life when I did not understand why my friends
could not help me. The Lord reminded of Psalm 55:22, "Cast thy
burden upon the LORD, and he shall sustain thee," and Isaiah 53:4,
"Surely he hath borne our griefs, and carried our sorrows: yet we
did esteem him stricken, smitten of God, and afflicted." I want to
encourage those who experience rejection that you are "heirs of God,
and joint-heirs with Christ; if so be that we suffer with him, that we
may be also glorified together. For I reckon that the sufferings of this

present time are not worthy to be compared with the
shall be revealed in us" (Romans 8:17–18).

For years, I dealt with individuals in the church who
of formalism. These individuals operated as if they were the only
anointed ones. They dissociated themselves from others, because
the truth of the matter is that they were really self-righteous, and
they only operated in their circle. It is amazing how they continued
to go through the whole process of protocol in the church setting. I
remembered that my mom had taught us at an early age that we were
special, regardless of how we were treated.

When I went to college and took a course in family dynamics, I
understood why it is so difficult for people to help you in a time of
need. They have been accustomed to pretending, and have not looked
within themselves to overcome their own personal issues.

When you experience what I call "church abuse," it will trigger
emotions that will negatively impact your life if you do not guard
your spirit. I struggled with the fact that no matter how faithful or
loyal I was to my employer or church, I was going to be scrutinized.
To be rejected is not a good feeling. I understand the scripture that
says your gift will make room for you. The problem was that I had to
overcome the battle in my thought process. In order for me to survive,
I had to ride it out, talking to myself and saying "Yes, it is difficult,
but I will get over it, accept it, and move forward."

Now I can freely talk about how I lived in silent depression. For a
long time, I struggled with the fact that I needed to look within myself
regarding my codependency. My problem was associated with me
being my family's scapegoat during my childhood. As a child, I was
not allowed to express my feelings; as result of this, I became emotionally isolated and had difficulty in confrontation. I would rather
listen to your pain than express mine. In my adult life, I have relationships problems, and sometimes feel unloved and lack confidence. I
never dealt with my childhood problems, and it was easier for me to
pretend that everything was a bed of roses. However, I had become
vulnerable and made the wrong choices in my relationships. I had
tried to resolve my unhealthy childhood experiences by wanting
the acceptance of others. I was disappointed in my marriage, and I

wanted a husband who could meet all of my emotional needs, so I began to feel self-pity and to suppress my true feelings.

I realized that my personal feelings regarding my marriage and the choices I made in my earlier years came out of my immaturity. However, as I matured, I learned that those bad choices not only affected me but also my family and friends. We say that God chooses our mate, but if this is the case, why did the person I chose end up being used by Satan to attack me? I clearly understand why. When we first met, he loved God, but because he was human, he allowed Satan to enter into his thoughts, and he acted out. Luke 11:24–26 says, "When the unclean spirit is gone out of a man, he walketh through dry places, seeking rest; and finding none, he saith, I will return unto my house when I came out. And when he cometh, he findeth it swept and garnished. Then goeth he, and taketh to him seven other spirits more wicked than himself; and they enter in, and dwell there: and the last state of that man is worse than the first." It is a known fact through this scripture that people backslide. This is why you have to guard your spirit. How do you guard your spirit? Through the Word of God.

Several years into the relationship, we divorced, but I started feeling guilty. I was sad and hurt, and I became depressed. Because of my mistakes, I found myself self-blaming and feeling isolated and unappreciative. When you feel rejected, it is human nature to want to belong. But God eventually gave me emotional insight that you do need healthy support, and that there is nothing wrong with getting counseling.

If you are experiencing hurt from family members, you need to step out and break away from your family. It's like bondage, and to break free, you need have to make a decision to let them go even though you love them. It is all about maturity, and God will bless you as you move toward a healthy environment.

We must build our own character, and it comes from our past and present experiences. God will allow you to be in the fire. Our character is not built of wood, stone, and plaster, but of faith, hope, love, and kindness. Your character is who you are. So every now and then, you need a self-inventory to be sure that you have rid yourself of anger and replaced it with forgiveness.

In this life, sometime your integrity will be attacked. I think of one devastating experience that happened at my place of employment. I was nominated as treasurer, and a few committee members accused me of stealing the money. I was personally attacked in the presence of other committee members. However, I had kept accurate records. Even though they knew their accusations were false, I never got an apology. It really hurt, especially when those who confessed themselves as Christians disassociated themselves from me. I continued to report to work and walked with my head up. My defense was that God would take care of the haters.

As I matured in the Lord, I've learned how to control my emotions. I don't address individuals when they wrong me. I am a firm believer that vengeance belongs to God. I just thank God that He has given me the spirit of discernment.

To have faith is to accept Jesus' testimony in His Word as true, and to rely upon it. Faith is to receive the Lord Jesus Christ into your heart. The definition of faith that God gave me is living in perplexity and knowing that God will make a way for you to escape. To make a way for you to escape simply means He will help you bear it. No matter if you are a single parent, a divorcee, or married, the Lord hears the cry of His people. In times of your distress, He will comfort you. Sometimes it is difficult to let go of past pain, anger, and resentment. If you want mental, spiritual, and emotional healing, you have to let go of the past. There will be no healing until there is repentance. You have to forgive the haters. The dynamic and true power of freedom comes when you change your heart. I am not bitter or resentful. My attendance at Sunday school, Bible study, and Sunday-morning services have equipped me. I am more skilled in God's Word, which sustains me during difficult times.

What I've learned, I can relate to those who are struggling with low self-esteem. I can identify with their struggles of thoughts of worthlessness, because I've been there. I know what it is to be divorced and to raise three children as a single parent. In the '80s, my ex-husband brought home $10,000 per month; that was a lot of money for twenty-year-olds. I drove a Cadillac Seville while in my twenties and had a nice home, but when I divorced because it was an unhealthy relationship, I lost it all. God is a restorer, and now I have been married twenty-five years to a man who loves God and his family.

I learned to rise above my self-defeating attitude, even though I was experiencing verbal, mental, and physical abuse. Where was God? He was there, because I did not lose my mind. I could have been institutionalized. If you praise God in the midst of your storms and keep your mind on Jesus, He will keep you in perfect peace (Isaiah 26:3). I kept quoting this scripture. Finally, I received my deliverance from people. I refuse to feel guilty because of the haters, because I know I am called, anointed, and appointed to win souls to the kingdom. Because of my confidence, I have been nicknamed by some of my church sisters and coworkers; they call me "May West," "Heaven," and "Movie Star." I am a star for Jesus.

I believe God put this book in my spirit in order to encourage you to be proud of who you are, because you are unique. Never allow anyone to make you feel guilty, or that you are not good enough. If you are a doorkeeper, a greeter, an usher, a teacher, or a helper in the church, your position is of great value and importance. Let your choice today be to get rid of frustration, fears, distress, and thoughts of despair that prolong behavior that causes you to feel inferior. You have to progress. Satan will try to discourage you and make you believe that you are not supposed to be anointed, talented, or gifted. I speak life into the situations that have stopped your spiritual growth. You will accomplish your aspirations and goals. Your children and family will be blessed. I rebuke all negative emotions. I pray that you do not allow things to overtake your real purpose of life. Remember that man's life does not consist in the abundance of things he possesses (Luke 12:15). In Jesus name, amen!

Chapter 8
A Celebration of Life

Queen Althea Tillman

Heaven-Sent, Heaven-Crowned
March 17, 1934–July 22, 2008

T his chapter is words of expression from my nieces, nephews,
aunts, and children that was printed in mom's obituary. She was
affectionally called Queen Althea and loved by many.

We surprised our mom and gave her a seventieth birthday celebration. We wondered how we could pull it off without her knowing.

One of my sister dear friend's daughter was going to be presented at a debutante on the same day. We told our mom to dress up because she was going to a debutante ball. Of course, we had to repent. I just want to share some of the writings shared by the family and with our mom at her seventieth birthday celebration.

WORDS OF EXPRESSIONS

To be a mother is to be a leader. Mother, you have been my spiritual leader, counselor, and mentor; you have taught me to put God first in my life. Having a spiritual mother is the best gift anyone could ever receive. I never heard you say a bad word, and I never saw you go out to party or even light a cigarette. Thank you for praying for me when I was asleep at night. Thank you for Tuesday-night prayer. Thank you for being there for me whenever I needed you. When I was a child, I remember you saying, "When I think of the goodness of Jesus and all that He has done for me, my soul cries out, 'Hallelujah!' I thank God for saving me." Now I'm grown, and those words will always stick in my heart. Once again, thank you so much for being a spiritual mother!

Mommy, I can't thank you enough for all the morals and values you instilled in me. I can't thank you enough for helping me to open my eyes, and for helping me grow into the fine young man I am today. I can't thank you enough for all your prayers and your continuous words of encouragement. I can't thank you enough for showing me that prayer really works, and the importance of being a God-fearing man. I can't thank you enough for making sacrifices to help better the lives of many. Really, I can't thank you enough for all that you have done for me in my life. Mommy, I will carry your blessings for the rest of my life. Even though you are not here today, I shall remember and cherish all of our memories and blessings, and even the whippings of yesterday. I will use what you have taught me each and every day. I will be sure to pass your blessings down to the generation of tomorrow. I will try not to live in sorrow or have a heart filled with sorrow. Mommy, you will truly be missed, but never forgotten; I will always love you, and I am proud that God chose me to be your grandson.

When I think of the goodness of Jesus, I think of Mommy. When I think of all that He has done for me, I think of Mommy. Mommy, words can't explain how much you mean to me. You have truly been an inspiration in my life. While growing up, I could never understand how someone could be tough and be loved by so many people. But now it all makes senses. You were a strong praying woman with a heart of gold. You are the true definition of being heaven-sent. Mommy, thank you for everything you have done for me and taught me. I am very thankful and blessed to have a grandmother like you!

When I think about you, I can see a beautiful smile on your face. You have been a blessing in my life, and you have been a great inspiration to me and others. God gave you the ability to be a wise mother to your family and to counsel others. You were truly a wonderful sister! When I think of my sister on this day, I'm reminded of a woman of virtue. Al, I will always remember you as a kind, loving, and caring person with a meek and humble spirit. You were a woman of great wisdom, and many lives were touched through your thoughtfulness.

Al, I will always love you. I know that I did not speak those words to you nearly as often as I should have, but I know that I made you laugh many times when you least expected it. Each and every time I made you laugh was another way of me saying, "Al, I truly love you." I will miss you, but I will think of your good and kind spirit forever.

Happy Seventieth Birthday to My Sister Althea

When I think about you, I can see a beautiful smile on your face. You have been a blessing in my life, and you have been a great inspiration to others and me. God has given you the ability to be a wise mother to your family, and the wisdom to counsel others. You are truly a wonderful sister.
May God continue to bless you and your family.

A Birthday Tribute to My Sister

When I think of my sister on this day, I'm reminded of a woman of
virtue. Al, you are a kind, loving, and caring person with a meek
and humble spirit.
You are a woman of wisdom, and many lives have been touched
through your thoughtfulness.
You are truly a virtuous woman. I pray that God will continue to
bless you.
I wish you a wonderful, happy seventieth birthday!

A Tribute to My Mother

To be a mother is to be a leader.
Mother, you have been my spiritual leader, counselor, and mentor.
You have taught me to put God first in my life.
To have a spiritual mother is the best gift anyone could
ever receive.
Growing up, I've never heard you say a bad word,
never seen you go out to a party or even light a cigarette.
Thank you for praying for me when I was
asleep at night.
Thank you for making sure I was in church
Every time the door was open.
Thank you for Tuesday-night prayer.
Thank you for being there for me whenever
I needed you.
When I was a child, I remember you saying,
"When I think of the goodness of Jesus and all that He has
done for me,
my soul cries out 'Hallelujah!'
I thank God for saving me."
Now I'm grown, and you're still saying the same words.
Those words will always stick to my heart.
Once again, thank you so much for being a spiritual mother.

A Special Tribute to Mommy

Before we could feed ourselves, you were there!
Before we could crawl, *you* were there!
Before we could walk, *you* there!
Before we could talk, *you* were there!
Before we could pray, *you* were there!
Before we could pray, you were there; pray for each one of us.
So that we could grow in the spirit of Christ Jesus our Savior!
So that we could be leaders and not followers!
So that we could call on the name of Jesus in our time of trouble!
So that we could overcome our disappointments!
So that we could achieve our goals and dreams,
knowing that we could do all things through Christ who
strengthens us!
Mommy, because of your prayers and fasting,
we are able to defeat the defiler and overcome our obstacles.
You taught us that a family that prays together stays together!
As obedient children, we listened and we learned.
Through prayers, we have grown strong as a family,
and we are gathered here tonight to honor you as our mother
and the strong rock of the Tillman Family!
With your love and spiritual guidance,
I was able to raise my children with strong values.
Now my daughters and my son may take what they
learned from me
and raise their children with the same spiritual guidance.
We love you, and we will always cherish your faithful commitment
to our family.
Happy seventieth birthday!

The Greatest Blessing

"She opens her mouth with wisdom;
And in her tongue is the law of kindness.
She looketh well to the ways of her household,
And eateth not the bread of idleness.

Her children arise up, and call her blessed."
Proverbs 31:26–28
There is a special bond between a mother and a daughter, at least there is between
me and you. Somehow, you seem to know what I'm feeling deep inside, no matter what I may say. You have always been there for me, and your love reassures me every day. There are not enough words to express my gratitude to you for all the things you have done. You're the best blessing that God have given me. I love you, Mommy, and I rise up and call you blessed.

Happy Seventieth Birthday

Today is one of the greatest days of my life. My mother is cele-brating a special day with family and friends. We have all been touched and inspired by this special angel of God, a mother, grand-mother, sister, and friend called "Mommy" by many.
Mommy took me as a child and planted the seed of God into my heart. I remember when I was ten years old, I would always think, "Wow, I have the nicest mother in the world." Thirty-two years later, I still think, "Wow, I have the nicest mother in the world." The most memorable time growing up in a house of twelve chil-dren was waking up to Mommy's loud verbal prayers to the Lord through the night, many nights for many years. Thank you, Mommy, for all of your prayers in the late hours of the night and early mornings of the day. Mommy, I want to thank you for all the praise songs you would sing as you were cooking and cleaning.
Thank you, Mommy, for the words of wisdom that you have instilled in me. Since I was a child, you have always given me your words of wisdom. You have given me Bible verses and encour-aging words to remember in my everyday walk of life, all of which keep me strong while facing good times or the unexpected difficul-ties of life.
I know for sure that you have been a great mother. I wish I could be as good a mother to my children as you have been to me.

A Grandmother's Love

You love me especially different than anyone else.
You are always there by my side in every step that I take.
Your honesty, intelligence, integrity, and love for God have made
you the best role model and grandmother that anyone could ever
ask for. There is no question of your greatness.
You are so awesome: I wouldn't trade you in for the world.
Thank you, Mommy, for all the things you have done for me.
I love you more than I can ever show you!
Happy birthday, Mommy.

Thank You!

Thank you is simply just words.
It's just a set of words that acknowledge how much I
appreciate you.
You are my strength, my backbone, my friend, and my mentor.
You have done so many great things for me that I want to just say
thank you.
I love you for who you are and what you have been to me.
There are not enough times I could say this, but thank you.

Happy Seventieth Birthday, Mommy

To be happy, you have to have the glory of God in your life. This is
just one of the very valuable lessons I have learned in my lifetime.
No matter what life has to throw at me, God will always be there.
When I was ready to give up on life, you were there to let me know
that everything was going to be OK.
Mommy, you prayed for me when I needed you to, and also when I
was mad and didn't want you to.
Mommy, I remember when you would get the blessed oil and put it
on my head, and you would "rebuke the devil out of me," as your
called it. When I was good and when I was bad, you never stopped
loving me, taking care of me, and giving me guidance. Mommy, I
want you to know that I could only remember a few times that you

have told me no. I want you to know that I love you very much, and I am extremely thankful for everything you've ever done for me. Mommy, thank you for teaching me to evaluate myself. You taught me to love myself and not to worry about what others think. You also taught me to always put God first. I love you, and thank you for helping me become the person I am today. Without you, I probably wouldn't even be here.

Mommy: How Could I Describe Her?

I can describe Mommy in millions and millions of words, but not one word would perfectly describe Mommy. That's why I'm thankful that the Lord put me in such a blessed family. Today we're celebrating Mommy's seventieth birthday. I know that I have not been on this earth that long, but over the past years, I've learned a lot about my sweet, dear grandmother, Althea Tillman, better known as "Mommy." Over the past years, I've learned that Mommy is a blessed, loving, gentle, sharing, willing, and giving person.
Over the years, my grandmother has helped me tremendously. Like, for instance, when I was feeling down and against the ropes, who could I turn to?
When I was feeling like everybody was against me, who could I turn to?
When I felt that I just wanted to die and that I could not trust anyone, who could I turn to?
Of course, I turned to my grandmother, Mommy, for some encouraging words that would brighten up my day. Everybody in this room knows what I am talking about, and I just want to say thank you, Mommy, for your support and your encouragement. You have truly made a difference.

Best Wishes to My Grandmommy

Grandmommy, when I was only five years old, you gave me a word from the Lord. Those words continue to grow in my heart. I'm now fourteen years old, and those few words have allowed me

to make better choices in education, athletics, and how I live my life on a daily basis.
Yes, I look to God to direct my paths.
Happy birthday, Mommy!

Happy Birthday, Grandmommy

A: Almighty
L: Loving
T: Truthful
H: Holy
E: Enthusiastic
A: Awesome

Mommy, you have a wonderful name, and you are blessed with so many beautiful characteristics. My favorite is "holy."

Who Is Mommy

Mommy is a combination of all things. She makes everything work out. Mommy is like honey to a bee, or water to a plant. To me, Mommy is like a teacher to a student. She knows right from wrong and wrong from right. Mommy has taught us young kids a lot. I don't know what we would do without her. When we do wrong, she gets us until we do right. But one thing I like about my grandmother, Mommy, is that she doesn't expect us to be perfect. Mommy is a loving and giving person. When we need something, she is always there to offer help.
Mommy is a person to never disrespect. If you disrespect Mommy, you are coming against a whole lot of nerve.
You might think of Mommy as no different from the rest of us, but I think of her as one of us, of course, and a trillion love bugs, with a heart as big as the Pacific Ocean.
Mommy gets invited to lots of different things, and she is always invited into my heart. It does not matter how many times she has to chastise me, I am proud of her, and I know that she loves me, because the Bible says that if you love a child, you will punish them. So every time Mommy punishes me, my heart gets bigger

and bigger, and I learned each and every time that Mommy is the key to success.

Happy seventieth birthday, Mommy!

Mommy, a Woman of Beauty

Mommy is a woman of beauty, inwardly and outwardly, who I adore. I am the firstborn of twelve siblings. I watched your life as you made a tenacious stand to make your family your priority. This is remarkable.

As I reflect on your life, I am reminded of Genesis 17:16, "And I will bless her, and give thee a son also of her: yea, I will bless her, and she shall be a mother of nations; kings of people shall be of her."

Mommy, the scripture refers to Sarah, who was called the mother of the families of the earth. God has blessed you with seven daughters and five sons. Well, Mom, you are a mother of many children.

You are my natural mom as well as my spiritual mom.

Mommy, you bring sunshine to brighten our lives because of your kindness, which is found in your warm, loving ways. You bring beauty and grace to your children. Your laughter brings gladness and warmth to all of us.

The sweet things you do are memories that we always will cherish. Throughout these years, you have been a blessing to me, and I am happy that God has chosen me to be your firstborn to witness your struggles and how maintain your integrity. The greatest characteristic of your life is faith. I learned from you because your faith underwent great sacrifices for your children.

Mommy, you are a model of hope and peace. You taught us to love one another, to be friendly, to think positively, to forgive one another, to have goals to achieve, and to have total dependency on the Lord. I'll always cherish and love you.

CPSIA information can be obtained
at www.ICGtesting.com
Printed in the USA
FSOW04n0027200317
31984FS